# THE LONDON
## DM AND DMS BUSES

# THE LONDON
## DM AND DMS BUSES
### Two Designs Ill Suited to London

JIM BLAKE

PEN & SWORD
TRANSPORT

AN IMPRINT OF PEN & SWORD BOOKS LTD.
YORKSHIRE – PHILADELPHIA

First published in Great Britain in 2024 by
Pen and Sword Transport
An imprint of
Pen & Sword Books Ltd.
Yorkshire - Philadelphia

ISBN 978 1 39903 474 6

Typeset by SJmagic DESIGN SERVICES, India.

Printed and bound in India by Parksons Graphics Pvt. Ltd.

Pen & Sword Books Ltd. incorporates the imprints of Pen & Sword Books: After the Battle, Archaeology, Atlas, Aviation, Battleground, Discovery, Family History, History, Maritime, Military, Naval, Politics, Railways, Select, Transport, True Crime, Fiction, Frontline Books, Leo Cooper, Praetorian Press, Seaforth Publishing, Wharncliffe and White Owl.

For a complete list of Pen & Sword titles please contact

PEN & SWORD BOOKS LIMITED
George House, Units 12 & 13, Beevor Street, Off Pontefract Road,
Barnsley, South Yorkshire, S71 1HN, England
E-mail: enquiries@pen-and-sword.co.uk
Website: www.pen-and-sword.co.uk

or

PEN AND SWORD BOOKS
1950 Lawrence Rd, Havertown, PA 19083, USA
E-mail: uspen-and-sword@casematepublishers.com
Website: www.penandswordbooks.com

# INTRODUCTION

WHEREAS LONDON TRANSPORT'S RT family and Routemasters double-deckers of the 1950s and 1960s were purpose-built for that operator, and enjoyed many decades of faithful service, thus becoming iconic London buses, their intended successor, the DMS, was the absolute opposite. Ironically dubbed 'The Londoner' when first introduced at the beginning of 1971, they soon became unpopular with passengers, operating staff and mechanical staff alike due to their unreliability, amongst many other things.

The 1960s had been a turbulent time for London Transport's buses. Services, especially in Central London, were increasingly disrupted by traffic congestion, thus leading to many routes becoming unreliable. A parallel headache for LT was caused by staff shortages, work on the buses no longer being as popular as it had been before the war, and despite staff being imported from Ireland, the Caribbean, the Indian sub-continent and elsewhere in the British Commonwealth, the problem persisted. This too led to cuts to services, often at short notice if existing staff members went sick, and so on.

The powers-that-be at 55, Broadway naturally examined various methods to address these twin evils bedevilling their bus network. By the 1960s, many British bus operators had seen one-man operation as an answer to staffing problems, and also as a way of cutting operating costs. However, it was only in the Country Area that London Transport used this method of operation to any great extent, from the mid-1950s onwards with RF and GS class single-deckers. As late as 1971, some 41-seat RFs in the Central Area still operated with a conductor, as did 39-seat examples on Green Line coach routes until very late in the 1960s. A considerable barrier to the spread of one-man operation was, of course, the bus staff's trade unions, who obviously wanted to protect their members' jobs, especially since female drivers on London's buses were not permitted until 1974, thus conductresses' jobs were particularly at risk.

Nevertheless, LT did resort to one-man operation in the Central Area as an answer to their staffing problems, whilst the curse of traffic congestion was to be addressed by the shortening of long routes, often with the inner section retaining crew operation and the outer section becoming a separate one-man operated route. Sometimes, very long routes were to be spilt into three or more sections. Although it was possible in some cases to introduce one-man operation with existing vehicles, the sturdy and very reliable RFs, by simply dispensing with their conductors on routes in the outer suburbs, even this of course met with stiff opposition from the trade unions.

Much more radical were proposals to introduce new high-capacity 'standee' single-deckers working new routes based on Central London main line railway termini or outer London suburban Underground stations. Other new high-capacity one-man operated single-deckers, but fully seated with a single front entrance/exit, were to replace double-deckers on existing suburban routes. It is important to note that when these proposals were formulated in the early/mid-1960s, one-man operation of double-deckers was not permitted, as they still were not when the plans finally came to fruition in 1968.

All of this culminated in London Transport's 'Reshaping Plan'. Various experimental types of vehicles were purchased for evaluation, entering service in both the Central and Country Areas in 1965/66, a time when Routemasters were still being built to replace the earlier generation of RT-types dating from the early post-war years. A prototype front-entrance, rear-engined Routemasters was produced, anticipating one-man operation being allowed on double-deckers, one of an intended four such prototypes to be used in both the Central and Country Areas to implement the 'Reshaping Plan'. Unfortunately, however, government legislation forced London Transport to discontinue its long-successful policy of having buses built to its own specific designs, and to buy 'off-the-peg' standard manufacturers' products just like every other operator.

Experimental types which entered service in 1965/66 included the XA and XF class double-deckers, having rear-engined Leyland Atlantean and Daimler Fleetline chassis respectively, and front entrance Park Royal bodywork, internally trimmed in similar fashion to Routemasters being built alongside them. Both types had been successfully crew-operated by many fleets outside London, and LT's eight XFs were sent to the Country Area at East Grinstead, having the novel feature of being able to shut off their upper decks at quiet times, effectively making them single-deckers and thus able to be one-man operated. Perhaps because they had similar mechanical features, notably their Leyland engines, fifty XAs were supplied to replace LT's existing fleets of RTLs and RTWs as well as some RMs, working in the Central Area at first on comparative trials with RMLs. The eight XFs were swapped with eight XAs, with which they worked alongside, also as part of these trials, in the latter half of the 1960s.

Once one-man operation was permitted on double-deckers, London Transport chose the rear-engined Daimler Fleetline as its standard type, mainly because the XFs had been more reliable than the XAs. The first of these were delivered in the autumn of 1970. They entered service at the beginning of January 1971, and despite the type having been successfully operated for ten years or more in the provinces, they proved to be an absolute disaster at London's service. Even the body design was viewed with disdain – whereas most traditional rear-engined double-deckers (including the XAs and XFs) had quite attractive bodywork, that on DMSs resembled an oblong box, thus earning them the nickname 'boxes on wheels'. An all-over red livery with no cream or white waistband did not help, whilst internally their blue and grey trim gave a cold impression, not helpful when the first of them entered service in mid-winter. To add insult to injury, they had the same split-entrance configuration as the already discredited SMSs, where passengers either paid the driver or put their exact fare in a slot in a machine to go through a turnstile. Most passengers distrusted using the latter, which often broke down anyway, leading to unacceptable boarding times and therefore longer journeys. The DMSs also suffered from repeated mechanical failures, notably to their rear engines which often caught fire, all a recipe for disaster. Many had ridiculously short working lives, the most absurd being DM931 at Cricklewood Garage, which managed only about eight or nine months on the road.

Naturally, the vehicles' poor performance was all the more galling to London Transport, who had been forced to buy these 'off-the-peg' vehicles thanks to government policy. If they had been allowed to have mass-produced front entrance rear-engined Routemasters like the solitary prototype, FRM1, things would have been a lot different.

All of this is illustrated and related in the pages that follow. It covers the DM and DMS types from their introduction until mass withdrawals of the class took place in September 1982. But for a change in management of the London bus fleet enforced by the Thatcher regime in June 1984, their final demise would have been in 1985, but since all-out one-person operation (OPO) was now the order of the day, surviving DMs and DMSs, mostly the later B20 type dating only from 1976-1978, had a stay of execution, lasting until the winter of 1992/93.

I have dealt with each of the two main single-deck vehicle types – the MB and SM – separately in a previous volume.

All of the pictures are, again, my own and most have not been published before. May I put on record my thanks to Colin Clarke for scanning all of my negatives, thus making this book possible, and to John Scott-Morgan of Pen & Sword Books for publishing it. I must also thank Ian Smith, from whose 'Ian's Bus Stop' website details of allocations and subsequent fates of the DMs and DMSs in their final years are derived.

*JIM BLAKE*
Palmers Green

**Above**: **The DMSs** that survived longest at London's service were the later 'B20' examples, by then produced by Leyland. This was largely because the government's restrictions on LT's activities forced them, from 1982 onwards, to replace RMs with new deliveries of Metrobuses and Leyland B15 Titans rather than the surviving DMSs. Before that happened, a somewhat careworn Bexleyheath DMS2273 sets off from Hare Street, Woolwich on trolleybus replacement route 96 for Dartford on 12 May 1980. It remained in LT service until November 1991, seeing three years or so with independent fleets afterwards before going for scrap.

**Opposite**: **The first** rear-engined double-deckers with front entrances to enter service with London Transport were the eight Country Area XFs. Three days after doing so, sparkling new XF8 from East Grinstead Garage collects passengers in Bell Street, Reigate on their designated route, the 424, on 21 September 1965. The fifty red XAs had virtually identical bodywork.

*Above*: **If London** Transport had been allowed to progress the design work they had done on the front entrance Routemasters, of which there should have been four prototypes, the unfortunate DMS class may never had existed. As it was, just the solitary prototype, FRM1, materialised. On a freezing 13 December 1967, it negotiates the roundabout at the southern end of Waterloo Bridge, working route 76 from Tottenham Garage. It had entered service on this route the previous July, but suffered an engine fire a few weeks later. Upon repairs, it was given standard Routemasters opening windows, having previously had forced air ventilation. The vehicle then had a successful operating career until the 1980s, when it was preserved. It still runs on special occasions for the LT Museum today.

*Opposite above*: **A strange** apparition passing Madras Place Cottages in Holloway Road on 28 November 1970, DMS1 is the first of what LT optimistically called 'The Londoner'. Its driver edges along gingerly, causing a long queue of traffic to build up behind it on this busy Great North Road. It is on driver familiarisation for route 271, which passed my home and to my outrage was the first route in North London to gain this type. Like them or loathe them, DMs and DMSs were an important part of London Transport's history, and this vehicle too is preserved at the LT Museum.

*Opposite below*: **On 15** January 1971, brand new DMS61 is also in Holloway Road, at the Nag's Head shopping centre, proudly displayed to locals on the day before route 271's conversion to the type. At least its external advertisements relieve its drab all-over red colour scheme. Of note is the new 'unfilled bullseye' symbol replacing the traditional gold London Transport fleet name, along with the symbols on each side beneath the windscreen, indicating that passengers could pay their fares in a slot machine on the nearside. Many of them will already be wary of this facility, having already suffered the dreadful MBSs on flat-fare routes at nearby Finsbury Park since September 1968. Moreover, having a friend in LT's schedules office who warned me several months beforehand of the 271's conversion, I had also warned all and sundry in my local newspaper, much to LT's public relations officer's disdain. My comments were dismissed with the excuse of 'teething troubles', from which of course the DMSs were to suffer throughout their short lives.

PRIVATE
EGP 1J

Holloway Road
Canonbury Road
City Road
271
HOLLOWAY ROAD
LONDON CHARLES DICKENS
MANCHESTER ASSURANCE
PAY AS YOU ENTER
MARKS & SPENCER
EGP 61 J

*Above*: **Things are** already starting to go awry on the morning of my local 271's first day of DMS operation, Saturday 16 January 1971. There has been a long gap in the northbound service when DMS54 finally arrives at the stop outside Essex Road Station. Will there be room aboard it for the elderly ladies who have been waiting patiently in the cold for the past half hour or so? The following Saturday, I was travelling south on one along Holloway Road that was likewise packed, and when an old lady alighted near Drayton Park, the doors closed on her arm which she was not able to remove. The bus then moved off, dragging her along, since the mass of passengers crammed into the vehicle's standing area prevented the driver from seeing what had happened. Fortunately, it was in heavy traffic, so the bus was moving only at walking pace and got caught at traffic lights soon thereafter, when the driver was able to be alerted and rescue her. Apart from being shaken, as was the driver, fortunately she was not injured. Sadly, that was not always so in many such incidents with these cumbersome vehicles, some of them fatal.

*Opposite above*: **Perhaps owing** to adverse criticism of their all-red livery, after the first batch of 117 DMSs had been delivered, those following had a broad white waistband applied. This improved their appearance considerably, as brand new DMS329 shows when outside Waterloo Station working a special service to and from the Ideal Home Exhibition at Olympia on 29 February 1972. A gold badge inspector on the right keeps a watchful eye on proceedings, including the photographer's activities.

***Below*: Quite early** on in the proceedings, following problems with the DMSs' fare collection equipment and consequent delays to other traffic, most of them were used on routes which did not pass through Central London. Typical of these is route 295, where they replaced RMs in June 1972. On the following 14 November, Wandsworth DMS344 has terminated in Ducane Road, East Acton as dusk falls. It is noteworthy how the 'coin-in-the-slot' symbols have been discontinued, a standard 'pay as you enter' notice being shown instead.

*Above*: **An oddity** of early one-man operation in LT's Central Area was the conversion of some routes at weekends only. This was in order to provide drivers on OPO services with sufficient weekend work, in this case those from the Monday to Friday only route 295. Thus, for a few months following that route's conversion, route 168 between Putney Heath and Farringdon Street was so worked on Saturdays, when 'to please the drivers' union' it was renumbered 168B. On the last day of this arrangement, 24 February 1973, Wandsworth DMS344 (by coincidence the same one illustrated above) sets off from the Stonecutter Street stand at the latter terminus.

*Opposite above*: **By the** spring of 1973, DMSs were again being produced in all-red livery. Two body makers were now producing them. In addition to the original batch (extending from DMS1 to DMS1247) bodied at Park Royal, Metro-Cammell were bodying those from DMS1248 onwards. A slight relief to the all-red monotony was the provision of yellow entrance doors, as recently-delivered Holloway DMS581 illustrates at Highbury Corner on 21 April that year. A revised 'solid bullseye' logo was also now introduced. Perhaps it has been allocated there to assist the route's original batch, which being more than two years old were already falling by the wayside.

*Opposite below*: **On the** same day as the previous picture, a well-filled and brand new DMS614 heads along Millbank on LT's Round London Sightseeing Tour. New DMSs were often run in on this service at the time before going on to their allotted use, replacing RTs and RMs on normal services.

red bus rovers
Holloway Road
Canonbury Road
City Road
271
red bus rovers
HIGHGATE VILLAGE
VISITORS LONDON
PLEASE PAY AS YOU ENTER
MLK 581 L

ROUND LONDON
SIGHTSEEING
TOUR
MLK 614 L

***Above***: **A week** later, on 28 April 1973, an earlier DMS still bearing the 'unfilled roundel' logo on the RLST is DMS1297, numerically the fiftieth of the first Metro-Cammell batch. It turns into Aldwych after crossing Waterloo Bridge. It would be instructive to know how many times these unfortunate vehicles broke down working LT's prestigious tour, all the more so what their passengers' reactions were when they did so.

***Opposite above***: **A departure** from the DMSs' original design in the latter part of 1972 was the fitment of some with double-leaf folding doors, rather than the four-leaf variety used hitherto. They were evaluated on route 278 which received them in October that year from West Ham Garage, and on 14 June 1973 their DMS464 illustrates this when passing through Plaistow Broadway. The feature was later adopted as standard for the class.

***Opposite below***: **On Sunday** 24 June 1973, brand new Metro-Cammell-bodied DMS1462 loads up at Uxbridge Station to take passengers on a free bus service to the Hillingdon Show. A bus rally formed part of the show, and the shiny new box-like vehicle must have been a marked contrast to older types displayed there. This DMS would not enter service until January 1974, having been used as a trainer in the meantime. It managed just over six years' service with LT, about average for the type, but achieved a further five years after sale to Lancashire United Transport.

HENDRIX
278
group4
MLX 464 L

HILLINGDON SHOW FREE BUS SERVICE
LETS GO TO
LETS GO TO
MLH 462L

*Above*: **On 21** September 1973, my camera catches another brand-new Metro-Cammell DMS, DMS1501, which has just negotiated the roundabout at Archway Station, heading into Holloway Road on delivery from Aldenham Works to Poplar Garage, where it too entered service in January 1974. It managed just five and a half years at London's service, though also survived to be sold to a new operator.

*Opposite above*: **On 10** April 1974, DMS827 is another new one being used on the RLST, and passes Blackfriars Station. Someone may be seen standing behind the driver – surely tourists are not being carried as standees? It is more likely that the person involved is a tour guide.

*Opposite below*: **Another instance** of DMSs operating specially at weekends to give OPO drivers work is route 19A, introduced on Sundays in July 1972 for those employed on Monday to Saturday route 39 on which DMSs replaced RTs. The route operated from Battersea Garage, working from nearby Parkgate Road to Tooting Bec Station. It replaced the daily 19 south of Clapham Junction on Sundays. DMS407 heads along Trinity Road, Tooting on 29 September 1974, its last day of operation. The 39 was reintroduced on Sunday the following week and this special route withdrawn.

red bus rovers
SIGHTSEEING TOUR
red bus rovers
red bus rovers
TGX 827 M

BATTERSEA
PARTS
MIDLAN

*Above*: **In the** autumn of 1973, largely because RTs were suffering certificate of fitness expiry more quickly than conversions of their routes to OPO could be implemented, routes 16 and 134 were converted to DMS operation, but retaining conductors. The RMs displaced were used to convert RT-operated routes, thus easing the pressure on requirements for that class. On 19 October 1974, Muswell Hill DMS1574 heads south along Muswell Hill Road on the latter route, shortly before new batches of this type were delivered as purpose-built crew operated DMs, with seating in the front section of their lower decks rather than the little-used automatic fare collection machinery. These released the DMSs on the two routes for their proper purpose.

*Opposite above*: **In addition** to large numbers of them, bodied both by Park Royal and Metro-Cammell, being delivered as crew-operated DMs (replacing RMs, which in turn replaced RTs, and sometimes RTs directly), most DMSs delivered during 1974/75 replaced the unfortunate MB and SM-type single-deckers instead of replacing RTs. However, on 12 October 1975, Holloway DMS64 is still soldiering on, working route 271, and for some reason has been diverted along Essex Road off its correct line of route. The vehicle has suffered a lot of dents on its lower front nearside. Owing to their flimsy construction, such damage often distorted their platforms, preventing the doors from working properly. This was another problem that kept so many off the road, in addition to engine failures.

*Opposite below*: **Somewhat peculiarly,** despite the fact that all of Edgware Garage's other routes had converted to SMS single-deck operation, their last crew-operated route, the 292, converted from RT to DMS in the summer of 1973. On 3 January 1976, DMS674 is still in use on this route when approaching Elstree & Borehamwood Station. It only ever operated from Edgware, being withdrawn and sold for scrap after just over six years' service. This section of the route, which still survives today, is outside the Greater London area.

271
HIGHGATE VILLAGE
EGP 64 J

JAWS
292
EDGWARE STATION
JAWS
MLK 674 L

*Above*: **DMSs often** suffered from overheated engines, leading many times to fires. The hot summer of 1976 did not help them, and on 12 August 1976, Wood Green DMS789 has come to grief, requiring the attention of the London Fire Brigade when working route 221, embarrassingly just around the corner from LT's divisional offices at Manor House. One of those initially used in crew mode on route 134, it did however manage its full seven-year initial certificate of fitness (CoF) spell at London's service, and after withdrawal in December 1980, spent a good few years in use in Hong Kong.

*Opposite above*: **The flimsy** bodywork on DMSs was not much help if they were involved in serious accidents. On 26 May 1977, DMS1976 and DMS2003 illustrate this outside Aldenham Works in the company of RMs some six times their age undergoing their third overhauls. Both, however, were repaired and just about managed their expected seven years' first CoF span at London's service, after which the former was sold for further PSV use and the latter retained as a trainer until the early 1990s.

*Opposite below*: **By the** late 1970s, when the last examples were still being delivered, London Transport had given up the ghost with their DMSs, with new Metrobuses and Leyland B15 Titans being delivered to replace them as their first seven-year certificates of fitness expired. A typical victim of that policy is Tottenham DMS431, which was withdrawn at that point (in August 1979) and sold for scrap. On 22 October 1978, it is at Edmonton, Angel Corner working Sunday-only route 279A, which had been introduced some five ...and a half years... earlier upon DMS conversion of the weekday 259. This was, however, this route's last day of operation. A week later, the 279A was converted from OPO DMS to crew RM operation, thanks partly to a barrage of public complaints about the DMS routes' appalling unreliability along the busy Hertford Road. This made history, being the first LT route so to convert, and it would not be the last.

PRIVATE
AEC

Tottenham
Finsbury Park
Angel Barbican
279
LOWER EDMONTON STN
advertise in
AL-ARAB
THE Top Rank CLUB
THE GLOBE
PLEASE PAY AS YOU ENTER
MLK 431L

*Above*: **Many of** these vehicles purpose-built as crew-operated DMs in the mid-1970s saw such use in North London, especially on trolleybus replacement routes at Holloway Garage. Most such routes, however, were converted back to RM operation during 1981/82. One that wasn't was route 17, which was withdrawn at the end of October 1978. On its final day, 27 October, Park Royal-bodied DM1053 is in the company of a Metro-Cammell-bodied example on the Archway Station stand at MacDonald Road. Route 17 was to be reintroduced in August 1985, and still exists today.

*Opposite*: **The ultimate** result of a DMS engine fire destroyed DMS1248, ironically the first of the Metro-Cammell-bodied examples, when working route 280 from Sutton Garage at Burgh Heath in the summer of 1978. Fortunately after its driver had safely evacuated his passengers, the fire quickly took hold with the results illustrated here. The wreck awaits disposal outside Aldenham Works on 2 November.

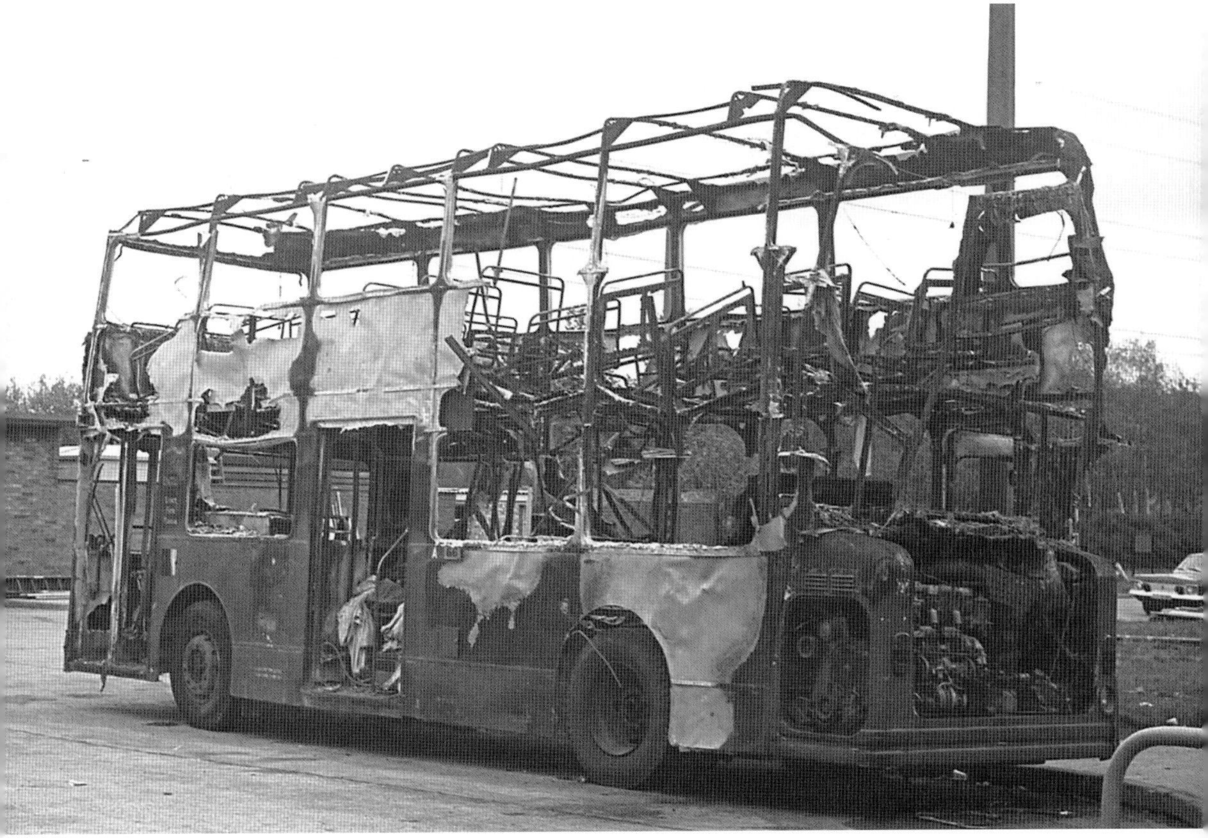

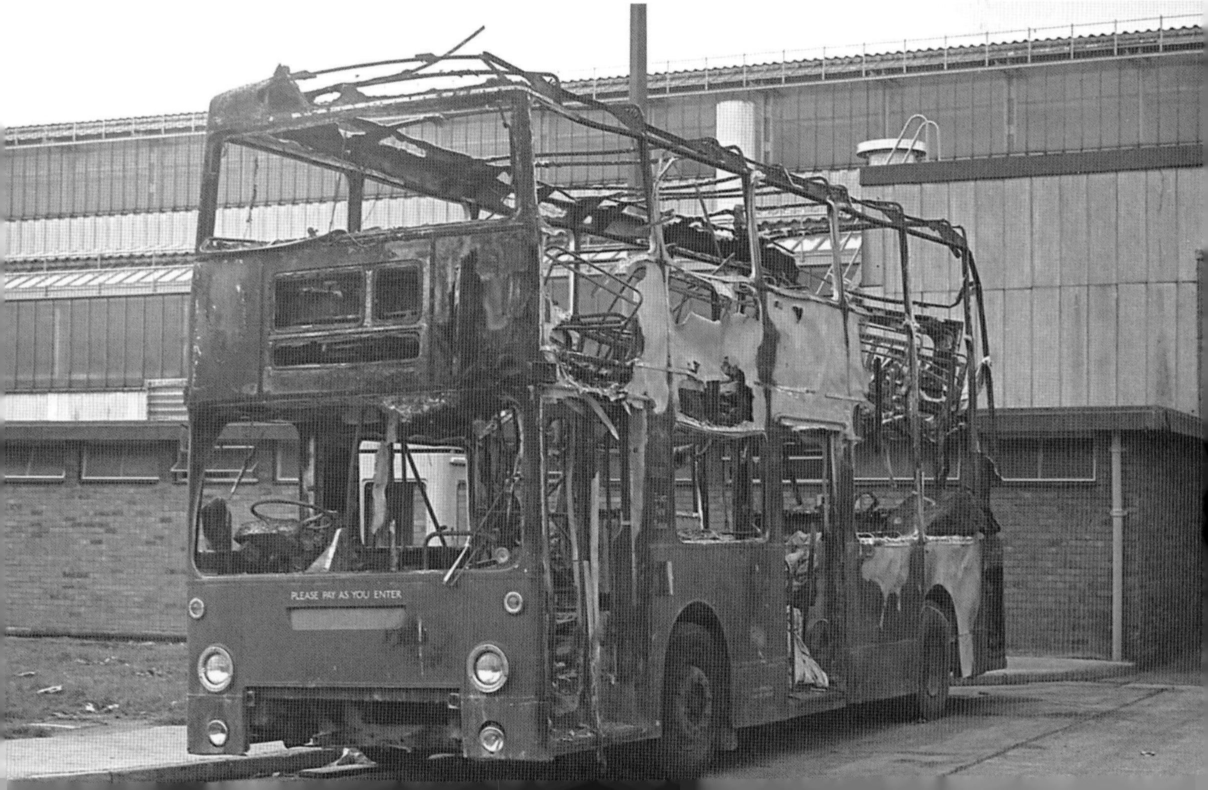
PLEASE PAY AS YOU ENTER

*Above*: **Six days** later, a defunct-looking DMS597 is being towed up Archway Road past Highgate Station by Ford Thames towing lorry 1987F from Holloway Garage, presumably to Aldenham Works for major repairs. It did, however, survive its seven-year CoF term, being sold after that and seeing a few more years' use in Lancashire. Such sights were commonplace when DMs and DMSs were at London's service.

*Opposite above*: **London's buses** still provided services on Christmas Day in 1978, albeit of a limited nature as they had for many years. On that day, Wandsworth Garage used their fairly new B20 crew-operated DMs, allocated for route 168, on route 28 instead of its usual RMs. DM2545 collects passengers in Kensington Church Street. In the event, this route was never to have a DM or DMS allocation.

*Opposite below*: **Starting on** New Year's Eve 1978, the last two months of the winter of 1978/79, we had the worst winter weather in London since the big freeze of early 1963. This was exacerbated by a strike of local council workers preventing roads being gritted. All of this had a disastrous effect on DMs and DMSs working routes in my part of North London, where they were unable to climb the steep hills on the Northern Heights. At lunchtime on 14 February, Wood Green DMS905 on route W2 is one of four heading north stuck at the summit of Crouch Hill. Another three were similarly marooned there heading south.

West Hampstead
Notting Hill Gate
Kensington Fulham
28
WANDSWORTH PLAIN
Thinking about insurance? GREAT!
Totally Hot
Totally Hot
BUS STOP
K
THX545S

Jetsave
BEST VALUE HOLIDAYS
USA
W2
TURNPIKE LANE STN
SMU 905 N

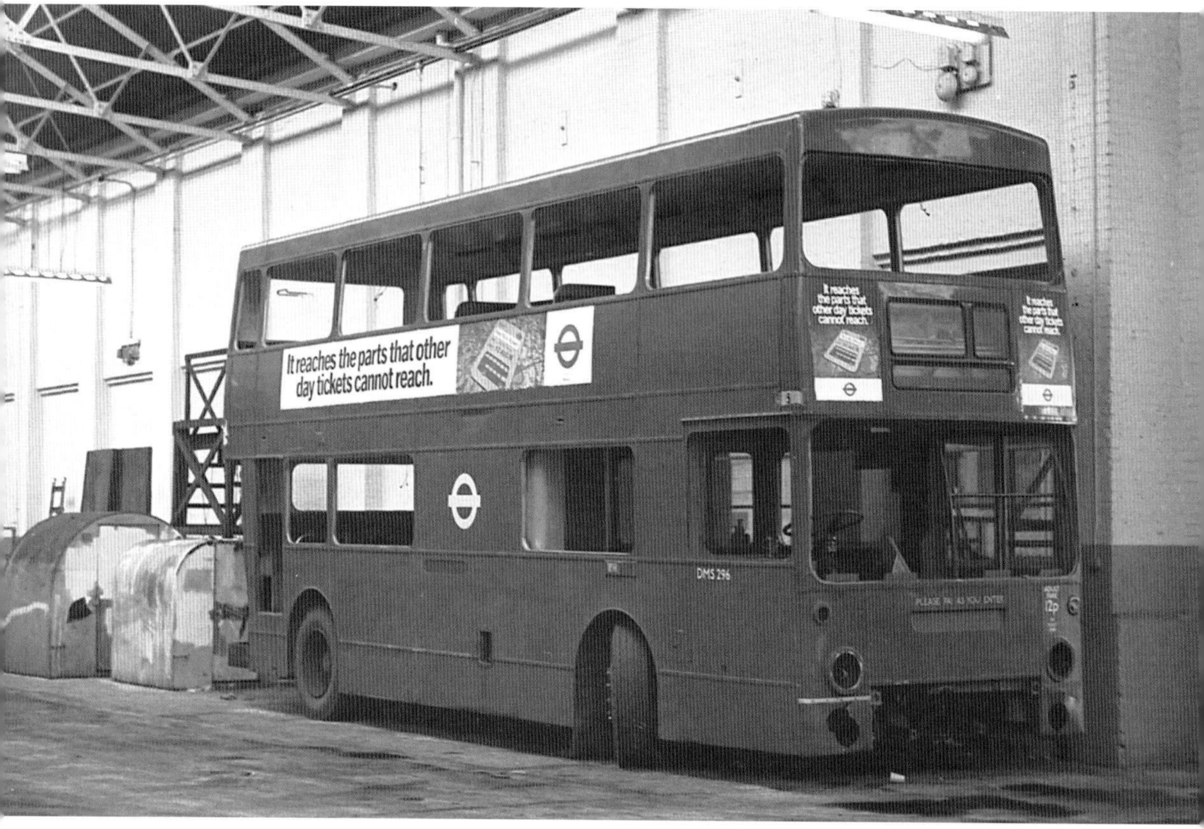

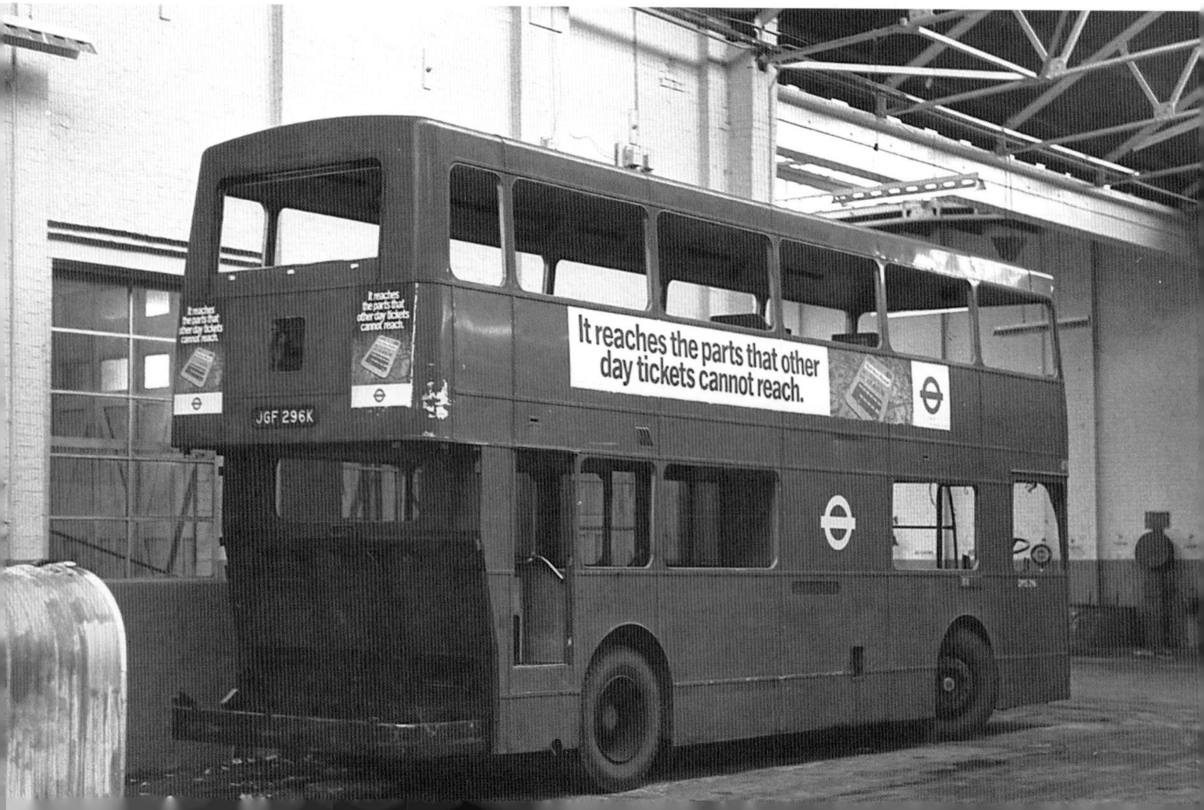

*Above*: **The ultimate** in *schadenfreude* for the many people who disliked the DMSs, me included, was when route 106 was reverted to RM crew-operation at the end of March 1979, after almost seven unhappy years using them. So unreliable were they on this busy inner-suburban route, operated by Hackney and Tottenham garages, that the service was sometimes almost non-existent. Ten days before the change, on 21 March, Tottenham DMS1405, at its Finsbury Park Station terminus, is only venturing as far east as Stoke Newington Common rather than continuing to Blackwall Tunnel for some reason. This would not be the last OPO route to revert to crew operation, either.

*Opposite*: **With deliveries** of new Metrobuses and Leyland B15 Titans coming on stream to replace the ailing DMS fleet as 1979 progressed, many DMSs were being withdrawn as a matter of routine when (and often before) their initial seven-year CoF expired. Some were sold for further service elsewhere, but others were stripped of spare body and mechanical parts to help keep others in service. On 18 March 1979, such a fate has befallen DMS296 in West Ham Garage and its gutted hulk awaits being towed away to the scrapyard. At this time, the last RTs were still in service at nearby Barking Garage, aged between 25 and 30 years.

***Above*: 1979 marked** the 150th anniversary of the first London bus services, operated initially by George Shillibeer, and London Transport commemorated it by adorning thirteen of their buses in an approximation of Shillibeer's dark green and yellow livery. Twelve of them were standard RMs from the final batch delivered early in 1965, the 'unlucky thirteenth' was DM2646, perhaps merely for *schadenfreude*. On 1 April 1979, it departs from Cricklewood Garage on route 16 for Victoria – I wonder if it got there without breaking down? This was the last of the unfortunate DM/DMSs delivered, new the previous summer.

*Above*: **For many** years, special route 137A ran the short distance between Sloane Square and Battersea Park at Bank Holiday weekends for the benefit of people visiting the park and Pleasure Gardens. On Easter Sunday, 15 April, Battersea DMS2227 arrives there. The white relief around the upper-deck windows on the final batches of DMs and DMSs improved their otherwise drab all-red appearance though did nothing, of course, to enhance their mechanical and structural unreliability.

*Opposite below*: **On** Good Friday 13 April 1979, one of these contraptions that will not reach its destination is Holloway DM1742, which has conked out at Manor House on the very busy inner suburban route 253. For the past four or five years, this RM-operated route had been worked at weekends and on public holidays by crew DMs from Holloway and Stamford Hill garages, but its third garage, Clapton, did not have any of them so always used RMs. When I was a conductor there on the 253 in 1974/75, it was noteworthy how many people, especially the many elderly babushkas in the Stamford Hill area who relied on the route, would ignore the DMs and wait for an RM to turn up – they hated the new vehicles.

*Above*: **At this** period, new offside advertisements that filled the panel behind the DM/DMSs' staircases, as well as the space between decks, also relieved the all-red drabness of these vehicles. Long before tobacco advertising on London's buses was banned, Holloway DM1053 on route 104 – another 'blessed' by them in place of RMs at weekends – turns from Canonbury Road into Essex Road on Sunday 13 May 1979. It is on diversion since Arsenal Football Club won the FA Cup the day before, and were on their triumphant procession with it along Upper Street to Islington Town Hall. Perhaps to confuse passengers further, the DM wrongly shows a via blind for route 172, one of its usual haunts during the week.

*Opposite above*: **During 1978/79** Route 244, which ran from Southgate Station to Muswell Hill with a rush hour extension to Golders Green (already linked between the latter two points daily by route 102), was officially allocated DMSs. On 23 June 1979, early DMS38 (which by now had had an Aldenham overhaul) is at Muswell Hill Broadway terminus. The route converted to LS operation next day, but as will be illustrated later, this type of double-decker would appear on it again.

*Opposite below*: **Next day,** 24 June 1979, sees Stamford Hill DMS136 on the terminal stand at Wood Green, Redvers Road, shared by routes 67, 243 and 243A. The 67 had been extended here three months previously, taking a much shorter route from Stamford Hill than the other two routes and covering previously unserved roads between South Tottenham and West Green to do so. This vehicle had also been overhauled at Aldenham, taking three months to complete at the end of 1978. It would be one of the dozens to perish as a result of the September 1982 Law Lords' route cuts, though it did survive to see use with other operators after sale by LT.

This space reserved for shrewd media buyer.
Phone 836 3456
Powys Lane
Bounds Green Station
Alexandra Park Road
244
MUSWELL HILL BDY
This space reserved for shrewd media buyer.
Phone 836 3456
PLEASE PAY AS YOU ENTER
EGP 38J
BROADWAY
TRAPEZ

RTS CENTRE
NTRE
THIN LIZZY
St Ann's Hospital
Stamford Hill
Dalston Shoreditch
67
ALDGATE EAST
Black Rose
THIN LIZZY
THE NEW ALBUM
PLEASE PAY AS YOU ENTER
EGP 136J

*Above*: **By now,** DMSs only a few years old could be seen alongside RTs thirty or more years their senior in the Yorkshire scrapyards. Such is the fate of Park Royal-bodied DMS512, not considered worth repairing after an engine fire a few months prior to its initial seven-year CoF expiry, at Wombwell Diesels on 5 July 1979.

*Opposite above*: **The Metro-Cammell-bodied** DMSs fared no better. The rear half of DMS1612 had been gutted thanks to an engine fire when working from Hendon Garage in February 1979, after it had seen just five years' service. It too is at the Wombwell scrapyard on the same day, with two SMSs that are only a couple of years older.

*Opposite below*: **So many** DMSs' CoFs were expiring at this time that many were sent to the closed Clapham Garage (used between 1960 and 1973 as the Museum of British Transport, somewhat ludicrously housing such large static historic steam locomotives as Gresley's world-beating A4 Pacific *Mallard*) for assessment as to whether to overhaul them, give them short-term recertifications, or sell them. On 9 July 1979, DMS400 and DMS401 are just two of a large number there. Their fates were markedly different; whereas DMS400 went for overhaul at Aldenham, took four months to do and was then withdrawn in the summer of 1982 anyway, DMS401 was immediately withdrawn and sold to Ensign in their capacity as a dealer, and was subsequently exported for further use in Hong Kong. DMS400 also went to Ensign upon withdrawal, but after languishing in their yard for a year or so, went for scrap.

The greatest name
in King Size
The greatest
JGF 401K
JGF 400K

*Above*: **On 14** July 1979, six-year-old DMS653 is in its final year of LT service when based at West Ham Garage. It heads south along West Ham Lane bound for the Victoria & Albert Docks on route 262, most oddly however working as a crew-operated bus. Following withdrawal, this one saw several years' further use with various British operators for longer than it did in London.

*Opposite above*: **By now,** so many CoF-expired DMSs were cluttering up LT premises that space elsewhere had to be found to store them. Not far away from route 262's terminus, DMS366 is amongst a group dumped at Royal Albert Dock on 17 July 1979. Sold to Ensign, it was used as a donor vehicle to provide parts for others they were refurbishing for sale to other operators, finally going for scrap more than three years later.

*Opposite below*: **After less** than three and a half years' use, DMS1906's hind quarters were destroyed by an engine fire when working from Potters Bar Garage early in 1979. On 2 August 1979, it is dumped outside Aldenham Works and was sold for scrap soon afterwards. Newer DMS2433 'next to it' had also suffered similar damage, as will be illustrated later.

It reaches
the parts that
other day tickets
cannot reach.
299
PLEASE PAY AS YOU ENTER
JGF 366K

The new
Suburbai
Bus Pass
Waltham Abbey
Waltham+ Cheshunt
Cuffley Potters Bar
242
SOUTH MIMMS
THE
WORLD IN
FOCUS
PLEASE PAY AS YOU ENTER
OJD433R
KUC 906P

*Above*: **Crew-operated DMs** had replaced RMs on busy route 29 in December 1975. They were not suited to it, especially through the West End, thus were switched to route 141 in March 1977, the RMs from that route replacing them on the 29. Wood Green Garage operated both routes, so they often subbed for RMs on it. On 4 August 1979, their DM1194 heads north at Spouters Corner, Wood Green bound for Enfield. The route had been extended and diverted to that point upon regaining RMs in March 1977, retaining them until November 1988. By then, DMs and DMSs were long gone in my part of London.

*Opposite above*: **Likewise, crew** DMs that had been allocated to busy West End route 24 were found to be unsuitable for West End operation, despite the trial batch of XAs having worked it reasonably successfully in 1965/66. Thus they were exchanged in April 1979 with route 18's RMLs and the 24 reverted to that type. The 18's crews at Stonebridge Park Garage had requested doored buses, since its stretch of route between the garage, Harlesden and Kensal Green was notorious for assaults and muggings of conductors robbed for their fare income. The DMs also worked trolleybus replacement 266, also running through the afflicted area, on Sundays. On 5 April 1979, DM1150 passes through Starch Green on its way from Hammersmith to Cricklewood.

*Opposite below*: **At Hammersmith** itself that day, Turnham Green DMS1476 loads up on route 267 in the forecourt of the former Metropolitan Railway terminus. This had been one of the final trolleybus replacement routes, in May 1962, and also an early RM to DMS conversion in September 1971. In June 1979, its majority allocation from Fulwell had been converted to Metrobus operation, with Turnham Green's following in December. By now, DMSs running basically north of the Thames were being squashed out of existence, with Ms replacing them from the west, and T class Leyland B15 Titans doing so from the east. This process started at the outer extremities and gradually worked inwards. Titans also replaced them in South East London, with South West London having the dubious honour of being the last bastion of DMS operation. The DMS pictured here, however, survived after sale by LT to be used for several more years than it had with them by several London sightseeing tour operators, as well as in normal service in Southend.

Willesden
266
CRICKLEWOOD GARAGE
KUC 150 P
LME 313C
It's worth it.
MAGNET

UNDER GROUND
267
HAMPTON COURT STN
PORRIDGE
Fletcher's inside story
MLH 476L
World proven Quality
CRAVEN "A"
59p
ALEX

*Above*: **Despite by** now finding use with other operators who seemed reasonably happy with them, DMSs continued to suffer frequent breakdowns at London's service. On 12 August 1979, Wood Green DMS770 has disgraced itself in The Roundway, at the southern end of the Great Cambridge Road, when working a 'short' from Turnpike Lane Station to Edmonton, Cambridge. Withdrawn upon seven-year CoF expiry just over a year later, it however saw further use in Hong Kong. Meanwhile, DMS1683 rescues its stranded passengers.

*Above*: **Before LT** gave up the ghost with its DMSs, an overhaul programme was begun for them at Aldenham. As with the equally ill-fated MB and SM-types, it proved impracticable for them to have body changes upon overhaul, in LT's time-honoured manner, thus prolonging their time off the road and adding to their already over-expensive maintenance costs. Thus, many were given two-year recertifications at Clapham Garage instead. One of these, DMS49, also a Holloway bus, has just set off from Archway Station for Waterloo on route 239 when passing the Whittington Hospital in Magdala Avenue on 16 August 1979. It saw further use in Hong Kong after sale by LT. Route 239 had originally run between Tufnell Park and King's Cross between 1934 and 1950, when it was replaced by tram replacement route 196. When RMs replaced that route's RTs in March 1971, it was reintroduced using SMSs and continued to Waterloo, the 196 being withdrawn north of Euston. Five years later, it received DMSs but converted to LS in December 1979. DMSs returned in 1981, only for the route to be withdrawn a year later.

*Opposite below*: **The low** bridge carrying the Great Northern main line over Stroud Green Road at the country end of Finsbury Park Station has claimed the roofs of many double-deck buses over the years. Few such incidents were as spectacular as that involving Holloway DM1757 in the evening rush hour of 14 August 1979. Fortunately, it was being driven back 'dead' to the garage by a fitter, after breaking down on route 4. As this view graphically shows, its flimsy upper-deck bodywork has been ripped apart by the impact, showering the road with shattered glass and other debris. The road is completely blocked, and the LS following on route 236 bound for Stroud Green is marooned. Remarkably, the fitter driving the DM had also deroofed an RML there only a few weeks beforehand. Whereas the roof of the RML had been cleanly peeled off, allowing it to emerge the other side of the bridge as an open-topper without even most of its upper-deck windows being damaged, the DM is well and truly stuck. The force of the impact also wrecked the vehicle's suspension, therefore after just four and a half years' service, it became the first crew DM to be scrapped. The deroofed twelve-and-a-half-year-old RML, in total contrast, was quickly given a new roof and returned to service, surviving until 2005.

***Above***: **One of** very few LT routes only ever operated by DMSs, the 296 was a special limited-stop service linking North Finchley, Tally Ho Corner with Copthall Sports Centre in Mill Hill. It called at Finchley Central, Hendon Central and Mill Hill East Northern Line stations on the way. It ran only from the end of March to the end of September 1979 and was funded by the London Borough of Barnet. On 25 August that year, Finchley DMS1934 has just set off on its circular trip as it heads south along Ballards Lane.

***Opposite above***: **During 1979,** the 'Shillibeer'-liveried DM2646 was 'rotated' to different garages in the same fashion as the dozen similarly-adorned RMs. Each was sponsored by various advertisers, and somewhat ironically, this DM advertises products by its own maker, Leyland, that are replacing the ill-fated DMSs – Leyland Nationals and B15 Titans. On Bank Holiday Monday, 27 August, it specially operates Muswell Hill Garage's weekend allocation on route 102 (normally working the 43 on Monday to Saturday and the 134 on Sunday) and has just departed from Chingford Station. One of the 'Shillibeer' RMs at Palmers Green Garage for route 29 also specially worked the 102 that day.

***Opposite below***: **All of** the flat-fare suburban routes originally operated by MBSs had them replaced by DMSs in the mid-1970s (except such routes as the S2 and S3 which passed beneath low railway bridges), but by the end of that decade, the DMSs themselves were on the way out. On 28 August 1979, Edmonton DMS821 heads south along Baker Street towards Enfield Town on route W8. This one actually survived to have an Aldenham overhaul early in 1981, only to be withdrawn less than eighteen months later as a result of the route cuts – of which more later. It saw further use after sale by LT as a London sightseeing bus.

TITAN
THE LEYLAND
NATIONAL
BRITAIN'S NO.1
SINGLE DECKER
Leyland Vehicles
102
GOLDERS GREEN STN
Leaders in passenger transport
THX 646 S

W8
PICKETTS LOCK CENTRE
TGX 821M

**Having initially,** as portrayed earlier, been operated with DMSs in crew mode, route 134 operated by Muswell Hill and Potters Bar garages later received purpose-built DMs, which had seats fitted in the forward part of the lower deck where DMSs had their AFC machines. On 10 September 1979, Muswell Hill DM1011 passes Archway Station heading south along Junction Road. Its conductor may be seen leaning against the vehicle's front. One very valid criticism of these contraptions was that, unlike on RT and RM-types, and even the experimental XAs and XFs, there was no 'cubby hole' under the stairs where the conductor could stand out of the way of boarding and alighting passengers when not collecting fares. This DM still looks very smart after a repaint a year or so before. Nevertheless, it was withdrawn following seven-year CoF expiry, never to run again after a year or so in store with Ensign Bus.

*Above*: **Things are** not as they seem on 28 September 1979, as Stockwell DM2612 heads south from Notting Hill Gate supposedly on route 168 bound for Farringdon Street. The route ran nowhere near this area, and in fact the DM is operating the Round London Sightseeing Tour. Presumably, one of those scheduled to work it had broken down and was hastily subbed by this one which happened to be in the garage. Oddly, it shows a via blind for the 155 rather than the 168, and since the sightseeing tour ran along part of these routes on Victoria Embankment, intending passengers for them must have been utterly confused.

*Opposite below*: **This view** of fire-damaged DMS2433 at Aldenham on 16 September 1979 shows just how destructive its engine fire was. Ironically, it was working from Ponders End Garage on route 107 which actually passed Aldenham Works when it happened. Despite all this, it was eventually taken in to the works for overhaul, emerging to Bexleyheath Garage in May 1982 three years after the fire had occurred – only to be withdrawn just three months or so later, and scrapped soon afterwards. It had entered service in July 1977, thus seeing only just over two years' service in total.

***Above*: Route 20,** briefly RT-operated for nine months or so when reintroduced in 1968 and then converted to 50-seat single-door MBs, was typical of those in the outer suburbs which had them replaced by DMSs in the mid-1970s. On 29 September 1979, Loughton DMS1688 rattles its way along Hoe Street, Walthamstow on its way to Debden. As related earlier, those in this area succumbed to Titans. This one survived until the summer of 1982, when many of them were swept away owing to the Law Lords' service cuts.

***Opposite above*: Further south** in Hoe Street that day, DMS3 of the original batch is not far from its home at Leyton Garage. It had had a full overhaul at Aldenham, taking several months, emerging to that garage in February 1978, remaining there until route 55 (on which DMSs had replaced RTs at the end of October 1972) reverted to crew operation using RMs at the end of January 1981. It moved to Upton Park, where it survived until withdrawal nine months later, never to run again. However, this DMS achieved more than ten years' service with LT, which, especially for their early batch, was quite a good innings.

***Opposite below*: Another early** DMS, DMS54, illustrated earlier when brand new on route 271, now looks more down-at-heel with a badly dented front. It is working from Peckham Garage on route 78, which had received the type to replace RTs in May 1972, at its Shoreditch Church terminus on 1 October 1979. It too had taken several months to overhaul and lasted until October 1981 before going for scrap.

London: How to go about it.
Clerkenwell Old St
Shoreditch Hackney
Lea Bridge Leyton
55
ALDWYCH
London: How to go about it.
SNOOKER
BILLIARDS
PLEASE PAY AS YOU ENTER
EGP 3J

London: How to go about it.
Liverpool St Aldgate
Tower Bdg Grange Rd
Peckham Park Road
78
DULWICH PLOUGH
London: How to go about it.
CLEEVE HOUSE
PLEASE PAY AS YOU ENTER
EGP 54J

*Above*: **On the** same day, at the other end of route 78, DMS503 arrives at its Dulwich Plough terminus. It still sports its original 'unfilled bullseye' livery, having never had an intermediate repaint since delivery in November 1972. It was withdrawn upon seven-year CoF expiry exactly seven years later, and swiftly despatched for scrap. Of note also is how the position of the headlamps has been changed since the original deliveries of DMSs exemplified by the two illustrated above. In February 1980, MD class Metro-Scania double-deckers, which had been delivered in 1975/76 as possible replacements for DM-types and initially used to replace RMs at Peckham and New Cross garages, replaced route 78's DMSs. The 36 group of routes at the same garage, on which they had operated, reverted to RM operation and basically remained so until 2005.

*Opposite above*: **The 194** was destined to be one of the last DMS-operated routes, retaining them until its garage, Elmers End, was closed in October 1986. However, DMS522, pictured at its Forest Hill terminus also on 1 October 1979, did not live long enough to tell the tale, being withdrawn and sold for scrap following seven-year CoF expiry two months later. It had spent its entire short seven-year life at Elmers End Garage, entering service to replace SMSs on this route in January 1973.

*Opposite below*: **MDs released** from their large allocation on routes 36, 36A and 36B at Peckham and converted for OPO also replaced DMSs at the old Plumstead Garage early in 1980, some also being kept at first as crew-operated buses and used to replace RMs on route 122, which were in turn swapped to replace MDs on such routes serving inner London. Route 122A had received new 50-seat MBs to replace RTs in the summer of 1969, later graduating to DMSs. Smartly turned-out Plumstead DMS1701 climbs up Woolwich New Road on 1 October 1979. Later used at Thornton Heath Garage, it was one of the myriad DMSs withdrawn as a result of the service cuts in September 1982, but survived to see several years' further use as a sightseeing bus in Chicago, USA.

JVC
The 'Tomorrow's World' of video recorders.
BEWARE OF THE SNAKE....
194
CROYDON AIRPORT
DMS 522
PLEASE PAY AS YOU ENTER
MLK 522L

London: How to go about it.
122A
WOOLWICH COM.
PLEASE PAY AS YOU ENTER
THM 701M

*Above*: **On the** same day, Abbey Wood DMS1472 is at Plumstead Corner on a short working on the outer section of tram replacement route 177 on which they had replaced RTs in January 1972. Their small DMS allocation on the route was also replaced by MDs upon their displacement by RMs at New Cross Garage in January 1981, but poor old New Cross Garage had to soldier on with DMSs for three more years or so until receiving new Titans. This one spent its entire seven-year working life at Abbey Wood, being used as a trainer for three years following CoF expiry in the summer of 1980 before going for scrap.

*Opposite above*: **Meanwhile, DMS** territory in the far west of London was soon to be invaded by new Metrobuses. On 2 October 1979, Southall DMS274 heads for home on route 282 at Greenford Broadway. This route had been introduced in November 1968 using new 50-seat MBs replacing the outer section of the 232, and subsequently received DMSs in September 1974. This one had gone to Southall after an Aldenham overhaul the previous April, and very soon after I took this picture was replaced by Metrobuses and transferred to Putney Garage. It perished there amid the September 1982 route cuts, too, never to run again.

*Opposite below*: **Also a** Southall bus, DMS1678 calls at Hounslow Central Station that day on route 120, which had received them to replace RTs in January 1978. It too was soon displaced by new Metrobuses, moving to a number of garages before withdrawal following seven-year CoF expiry in 1981. It saw a few years' further use with various new UK owners thereafter.

Greenford Yeading
Northolt Eastcote
Joel St. Northwood
282
SOUTHALL GARAGE
Packed with homes, holidays & businesses
Daltons Weekly
Every Thursday
Boots
DMS 274
PLEASE PAY AS YOU ENTER
JGF 274K

120
HOUNSLOW HEATH
YOU!
PLEASE PAY AS YOU ENTER
THM 678M

*Above*: **Uxbridge DMS1355** arrives at Hounslow Bus Station on the same occasion, with blinds already set for return to its home area on route 222. It had been new to replace SMSs on this route in January 1973, being withdrawn a few days after I took this picture, only ever having operated from Uxbridge Garage. It saw a couple of years' further use with West Midlands PTE. Meanwhile, Metrobuses replaced DMSs on this route in the summer of 1981.

*Opposite*: **Laying over** at Hounslow Bus Station that day, Southall DMS583 awaits departure for Yeading on route 232. It too was displaced by new Metrobuses (one of which is visible on the left) a few days later, moving to Sutton Garage from where it was withdrawn upon initial seven-year CoF expiry in March 1980. It never ran again.

*Above*: **On 7** October 1979, withdrawn DMS482 is one of two caught by my camera at Edmonton Cambridge roundabout on its way from Aldenham Works to Ensign Bus at Rainham, who had just bought them. Withdrawn the previous month, it had spent its entire LT working life (just short of its initial seven-year CoF span) working from Romford, North Street Garage which, by coincidence, operated routes in the Rainham area. It was later exported for further use in Hong Kong.

*Opposite above*: **Still working** from Romford North Street Garage on 20 October 1979 is DMS1877, loading up on route 66 at Leytonstone, Green Man Bus Station. New Titans were invading DMS territory in the East, too, though this one spent another eleven months at Romford before being moved on. It received an Aldenham overhaul ahead of seven-year CoF expiry in the spring of 1981, only to be demoted to training duties in the autumn of 1983 and sold six months later. It then saw a few years' domestic non-PSV use.

*Opposite below*: **On the** same day, Upton Park DM1065 (whose conductor may be seen in the front of the vehicle) has just set off from route 101's Wanstead Station terminus. This busy East End route had converted from RM to crew DM operation just under a year previously, and their use on it was extremely unpopular with crews and passengers alike. Thus, a couple of days after I took this picture, the route reverted to RM operation, remaining so until OPO conversion using new Titans in September 1982. This DM was transferred to Holloway where it expired a couple of years later, a few months ahead of its initial seven-year CoF expiry. It did, however, survive to see further use in Hong Kong.

Sansui sounds superb.
CLIFF RICHARD
66
HAROLD WOOD STN
MULTI-RIDE
DMS 877
GHM 877N

VALLIER
CHOPIN
101
EAST HAM
GHV 65 N

*Above*: **'Shillibeer'-liveried DM2646's** last allocation in this guise was at Brixton, for route 133. It changes crew outside the garage on 21 October 1979. It was repainted red in January 1980, and moved away from Brixton when route 133 converted from DM to RM operation in August 1981. The route had been converted direct from RT to DM in March 1975. DM2646 latterly became an OPO vehicle, remaining at London's service until 1992. After that it passed into preservation, regaining 'Shillibeer' livery.

*Opposite above*: **By this** time, of the flat-fare routes introduced in the Wood Green area upon 'Reshaping' on Saturday, 7 September 1968, only the W2, W3 and W4 still existed. DMSs had replaced their MBSs in the autumn of 1974, and some five years later on 23 October 1979, Wood Green DMS1663 crosses the junction of Turnpike Lane and Clarendon Road in Hornsey on route W2's circuitous journey to Finsbury Park. Local passengers, such as me, would have to suffer another two years of them before they, in turn, were ousted by new Metrobuses. This DMS barely survived its initial seven-year CoF period, never to run again after withdrawal.

*Opposite below*: **Stratford Circular** flat-fare route S1, which had replaced route 272 with MBSs in the summer of 1969, had a similar allocation history. West Ham DMS351 has just departed from Stratford's awful 1973-built original bus station (topped by a multi-storey car park) when running back to its garage on 10 November 1979. Upon seven-year CoF expiry, it had been locally recertified there, but perished after 4 September 1982, when hundreds of London's buses – including the first 200 or so RMs to be withdrawn in normal circumstances – became surplus to requirements thanks to merciless service cuts imposed on LT by the government of the day. It too never ran again.

Priory Rd Park Rd
Crouch End Broadway
Stroud Green Road
W2
FINSBURY PARK STN
PLEASE PAY AS YOU ENTER
ADULT FARE 15p
THM 663M

London: How to go about it.
STRATFORD CIRCULAR
S1
JGF 351K
SAXBY LTD

*Above*: **Further to** the east that day, Romford North Street DMS2148, bearing the later 'white upper-deck window surround' livery, collects passengers at Chase Cross terminus for a trip through outer suburbia to Rainham on route 103. This converted to Titan a few days later, displacing this DMS across the water to Catford. However, despite being still within its original seven-year CoF, it too was withdrawn amid the September 1982 cuts. It would later be drastically rebuilt as a coach (and also reregistered) operating 'luxury' coach tours in London for a few years afterwards.

*Opposite*: **In Romford** itself on the same day, North Street DMS1870 is very full of passengers when working route 294. Of note are the 'Multi-Ride' stickers on DMSs in this area, denoting an experimental pre-paid ticket scheme designed to reduce boarding times. It was in some ways a forerunner of today's Oyster Card system. This DMS too was ousted by Titans at Romford early in 1980, but would eventually see the best part of ten years' use as a trainer with LT.

*Above*: **Also in** Mercury Gardens, Romford that day, North Street DMS406 contrasts with a B15 Titan operating route 165 from Hornchurch Garage. It had arrived at North Street from Aldenham overhaul in October, being transferred to distant Sutton after displacement by Titans in February 1980. But it too was withdrawn in September 1982. It was eventually exported for further use in Hong Kong.

*Opposite above*: **On 25** November 1979, Park Royal-bodied DMS689 and Metro-Cammell-bodied DMS1459 make a sad pair in the yard of Barking Garage. Both had been new in the summer of 1973, the former only ever having worked at Barking and the latter also having spent most of its life there. One appears to have suffered accident damage, whilst the other has been stripped for spares and is a gutted hulk. Both went directly to Wombwell Diesels for scrap a few days later.

*Opposite below*: **Still in** the land of the living on New Year's Eve 1979, Barking DMS247 has just called at Becontree Station on its way from Ilford to Dagenham on route 145. DMSs had replaced RTs on this route in March 1974, this one having arrived at Barking the previous April after a light overhaul at Aldenham. Displaced by new Titans at Barking in June 1980, it moved south to Catford, being withdrawn in March 1982, never to run again.

Red Bus Rover 1,700 miles £1.10p
HISTORY IN THE MAKING
THE WORLD IN FOCUS
PLEASE PAY AS YOU ENTER

Green Lane
Bennetts Castle Lane
Becontree Heathway
145
DAGENHAM
A Cheap Day Tube Return saves getting the car out
PLEASE PAY AS YOU ENTER
JGF 247K

**Busy route** 43 had been one of the several in North London to convert from Routemasters to crew DM operation in 1974/75. On 24 January 1980, Muswell Hill DM1021 has been unusually curtailed at Archway Station, and is on the MacDonald Road stand there. Its crew have probably adjourned to the nearby staff canteen. This DM moved south to Thornton Heath when displaced by newer B20 examples at Muswell Hill later in the year but perished upon seven-year CoF expiry early in 1982, being yet another never to run again thereafter.

**Operated by** Thornton Heath Garage, DMS1424 has terminated at Mitcham Fair Green on route 64 on a very wintry 26 January 1980. Upon seven-year CoF expiry two months later, it was fortunate enough to be sent to Aldenham for a three-year recertification, yet was withdrawn anyway in the summer of 1982. It survived to see several years' further use with Ensign Bus and subsidiaries as a sightseeing bus in London, even working under contract to London Buses on route 145 in 1986/87.

**For several** years towards the end of its existence, the original route 23 through the East End was crew operated on Mondays to Saturdays, but OPO on Sundays. On Sunday 10 February 1980, Upton Park DMS1460 approaches the junction of the Barking Road and Greengate Street. It was withdrawn two months later as seven-year CoF expiry approached , but survived to see service in Lancashire and the Midlands for a couple of years longer than it managed in London.

*Above:* **During the** 1970s, LT introduced two 'express' bus routes roughly following existing trunk routes from Central London to the suburbs. Both were initially operated by flat fare MBSs. One, the 615 between St. Paul's and Poplar, lasted only a year or so, but the other, the 616 from Oxford Circus to Cricklewood, lasted much longer. DMSs replaced its MBSs in 1974, and survived into the early 1980s when Metrobuses replaced them. Eventually, the route was withdrawn and replaced by a diversion of route 16A, by then converted from crew DM to RML operation, to Oxford Circus instead of Victoria. On 29 February 1980, prototype B20 DMS854 is at Marble Arch. It survived in service until 1983.

*Opposite above:* **Trolleybus replacement** route 149, shared between Edmonton and Stamford Hill garages, converted from RM to crew DM operation in February 1974. Sharing its route with Routemasters-operated services 76, 243/A and 279, it was often shunned by passengers, as this view of an almost empty Edmonton DM968 in Fore Street, Upper Edmonton on 29 March 1980 perhaps illustrates. The unhappy DMs on the route were replaced by the RCL class former Green Line coaches, reacquired from London Country and overhauled as red buses, in the latter half of 1980. This one was new to the route, and prematurely withdrawn and sold to Hong Kong as a result.

*Opposite below:* **Route 149** was not the only crew DM-operated route on which they were replaced by Routemasters reacquired from London Country. In May 1980, routes 16 and 16A received mostly former LCBS RMLs for the purpose, too. On 8 April, Cricklewood DM2603 crosses the junction of Edgware Road and Sussex Gardens bound for Victoria on route 16A. This route had been newly introduced with crew DMs early in 1976 to serve the new Brent Cross Shopping Centre and had never previously been officially RM or RML operated. In common with those new previously to the 16, its DMs were replaced by the newer B20 variety like this one in 1978. Redeployed to replace earlier DMs at Muswell Hill on routes 43 and 134, this one was again ousted by RMs and RMLs in September 1982, then moving to Sutton Garage to work as an OPO vehicle, lasting until late 1991.

YAMAHA MOTORCYCLES
149
STAMFORD HILL
DM968

16A
VICTORIA
THX603S
RATTORIA
ADRIATICA

*Above*: **A crew-operated** route which did not lose its DMs at this period was the 18, whose crews insisted on retaining doored vehicles thanks to the feral youths terrorising much of its route. On 12 April 1980, Stonebridge Park DM1144 has just negotiated the one-way system at Warren Street Station when heading west. It had previously served this area on route 24 and ended its LT career at New Cross Garage. After sale, it spent a few years with independent operators in South Wales.

*Opposite above*: **On the** same day, a Saturday, Stamford Hill DM1736 turns out of Gower Street to reach route 253's Warren Street Station terminus working their weekend allocation of the type. New to that garage for the 149, upon displacement by RCLs it moved up the route to Edmonton, remaining as a spare for them until premature withdrawal in May 1981. It saw a few more years' service after sale with Midland Red and its successors.

*Opposite below*: **Also on** 12 April 1980, Cricklewood DMS2499 heads north up the Edgware Road between its garage and the former Brent marshalling yards and Cricklewood engine shed on the Midland main line on route 32. It is turning short at Colindale, rather than running the full route from Co. Kilburn Park to Edgware. Route 32 had been an early victim of the DMS, in March 1971, its original specimens having long since been replaced by B20s like this one. It migrated to South London after replacement by new Metrobuses in July 1980, ending up as a trainer in the early 1990s and then seeing further use in the Southend area.

Camden Town
Finsbury Park
Clapton Hackney
253
WARREN ST STN
SMU736N

Cricklewood
W Hendon Colindale
Burnt Oak
32
COLINDALE
THX499S

*Above*: **Whereas crew-operated** DMs made their debut at Holloway Garage in January 1975, they only at first worked route 4 on Saturdays. However full conversion (direct from RT operation) took place the following June. On 14 April 1980, DM1001 is on diversion away from Blackstock Road owing to another of the class breaking down and blocking traffic in both directions, and turns from Monsell Road into Plimsoll Road in order to reach Finsbury Park Station. It only ever operated from Holloway Garage, and when route 4 was converted to RM operation in January 1981, it was prematurely withdrawn. It saw a few years' further service with various independent operators in the late 1980s.

*Opposite above*: **Route 182** began life in the summer of 1970, replacing the outer section of route 18 and SMS-operated. As with most such routes (other than those with low bridges), it graduated to DMS and on 10 May 1980, Alperton DMS705 is at Sudbury, Swan heading for Brent Cross, to which point the route had by now been extended. Upon replacement by new Metrobuses in June, it too was banished south of the water, but then received a three-year repaint and recertification at Aldenham. After CoF expiry in 1983, it was sold for scrap, having achieved almost exactly ten years' service. Although quite respectable by DMS standards, this was of course a far cry from the long service lives of RT and RM-types.

**Sister vehicle** DMS704, also from Alperton, has terminated at Wembley Arena on route 92, on which the type had also replaced SMSs. This one, however, was withdrawn upon initial seven-year CoF expiry shortly after exile south of the Thames in July. It ended up as a staff canteen and rest room for an Essex independent operator.

*Above*: **Also an** Alperton bus, DMS1498 calls at Wembley Park Station on the same day. They had replaced 50-seat MBs on route 297, and this one was banished to the East upon being ousted by Metrobuses in June, later getting a three-year repaint and recertification at Aldenham. However, it was withdrawn just two years later, never to run again.

*Opposite above*: **Another DMS** on route 297 actually managed to convey me to Willesden Garage without breaking down. Arriving there too is one of its garage-mates, a rather careworn-looking DMS160 on route 226, another route on which they had replaced SMSs. It had taken six months to overhaul in the summer of 1978 (required owing to initial seven-year CoF expiry) and was another banished over the water to Walworth, upon replacement by new Metrobuses in June 1980. It was withdrawn in October 1982, never to run again.

*Opposite below*: **Entering service** at Chalk Farm Garage in the autumn of 1975 to replace RMLs on route 24, DM1157 moved to Muswell Hill upon their return to the route in the spring of 1979. On 11 May 1980, it trundles along Silver Street, Edmonton on their Sunday allocation on route 102 and appears to be well-filled. Displaced by newer B20 DMs ousted by RMLs on routes 16 and 16A a few days later, it was sent to Uxbridge Garage for route 207, where it was withdrawn in August 1981 after being replaced by Routemasters for a third time. It later saw use as a sightseeing bus in London and was then exported to the USA.

CAGNEY
CASUALS · SHIRTS AND SWEATERS
The Vale
Pennine Drive
Claremont Road
226
WILLESDEN GARAGE
COURAGE
DMS 160
PLEASE PAY AS YOU ENTER
JGF 160K

102
CHINGFORD STATION
KUC 157 P

*Above:* **Later the** same day, Abbey Wood DMS1681 crosses the Southern Region Dartford Loop at Plumstead Station, working route 272. This was one of a number of services introduced to serve the GLC's growing Thamesmead Estate, built on Plumstead Marshes. It was new to Abbey Wood in the autumn of 1974, after taking part in London's Lord Mayor's Show, presumably representing 'London's Bus of the Future'. That future was to be very short indeed, since it was displaced from Abbey Wood by Metrobuses in January 1981 and sent to the East, seeing six months' further use at Poplar before withdrawal upon seven-year CoF expiry. After sale, it saw brief use at Ensign Bus.

*Opposite above:* **Deeper into** suburban South East London next day, on 12 May 1980, Catford DMS2002 heads along Court Road, Mottingham on route 124. DMSs had ended this route's very short-lived period of RM operation (since July 1971) in January 1972. This one, however, had arrived there when new in the summer of 1976 to replace SMs on route 160. It was overhauled at Aldenham in the autumn of 1981, but was displaced at Catford Garage by newer B20 DMSs amid the cuts of September 1982. It survived almost another year at various garages before withdrawal the following summer but went on to serve a variety of operators until the late 1990s. Meanwhile, Catford's DMSs were swept away by new Titans in the summer of 1983.

*Opposite below:* **On 13** May 1980, locally-based DM2625 crosses Cricklewood Broadway on a short working of the 16 trunk route to Co. Kilburn Park Station. When RMLs replaced these vehicles on routes 16 and 16A a couple of weeks later, it moved to Muswell Hill and, following replacement there too by Routemasters on routes 43 and 134 amid the September 1982 changes, was converted for OPO use. New in June 1978, it lasted until the spring of 1992 serving at such South London garages as Thornton Heath, South Croydon and Sutton. It saw brief use with an independent operator after sale later that year.

London: How to go about it.
Falconwood Eltham Mottingham Grove Pk Catford Perry Vale
124
CATFORD
London: How to go about it.
YAMAHA MOTORCYCLES
DMS 2002
PLEASE PAY AS YOU ENTER
KJD 2P

Marble Arch Maida Vale Kilburn Cricklewood
16
KILBURN PARK STN
THE MAIL ORDER HOUSE
CRICKLEWOOD LANE
THX 625S

*Above*: **Eleven days** later, the DMS in the previous picture is working sister route 16A amid a group of others which have terminated at Brent Cross Shopping Centre on 24 May. Nearest the camera is Hendon DMS1565, turning short at Finchley, Manor Cottage Tavern rather than going through to Archway. It had entered service at that garage in January 1975 replacing RTs on route 183 after a year or so on training duties; those on route 143 having replaced the ill-fated 50-seat MBs. Metrobuses in turn ousted them in June, this one being retired upon initial seven-year CoF expiry in the autumn. It was one of the many subsequently exported to Hong Kong.

*Opposite above*: **For an** open day at Walthamstow Garage on 31 May 1980, DMS1487 has a full load of spectators when giving rides through the automatic bus-washing facility. I sincerely hope its windows did not leak – they certainly often did on these vehicles, especially at the front on their upper decks, in wet weather. It replaced RTs on route 144 (for which it is blinded) when six months old in January 1974, and was withdrawn upon initial seven-year CoF expiry in July 1980. After sale, it achieved eleven years' municipal service in Cheshire, illustrating how these vehicles often performed much better in the provinces than they did in London.

*Opposite below*: **In London** Transport days, Potters Bar Garage's buses were always well turned out, and on 12 June 1980 their DMS1895 at South Mimms, White Hart on route 242 looks very smart indeed. New to the garage in August 1975 to replace 50-seat MBs on this route, it has just been repainted, and would stay there until Aldenham overhaul in September 1981. Outshopped to New Cross Garage three months later, it was withdrawn in the autumn of 1983, and never ran again.

LONDON TRAN
Go wherever you want with a Red Bus Rover Ticket.
144
WALTHAMSTOW
Go wherever you want with a Red Bus Rover Ticket.
MLH 487L

Waltham Abbey
242
SOUTH MIMMS
GHM 895N

*Above:* **Another that** had entered service at Hendon Garage for the DMS conversion of route 183, DMS1562 has recently been transferred to Ponders End when heading along Carterhatch Lane, Enfield on route 231 on 24 June 1980. Displaced there by B20 DMSs a couple of weeks later, it was exiled to Abbey Wood, only to be withdrawn in October upon initial seven-year CoF expiry. It was later exported to Hong Kong.

*Opposite above:* **On sister** Great Cambridge Road route 217, very full DMS38 calls at the second stop north of The Cambridge roundabout on 27 June 1980. It is working a scheduled afternoon journey terminating at Enfield Halfway House (aka 'Carterhatch') catering for homegoing workers from the factories along the Great Cambridge Road. Only transferred to Ponders End in May, it also was displaced by B20s in July, moving on to West Ham Garage where it lasted until withdrawal in November 1981. It went for scrap a year later. The vehicle had had a long-drawn-out overhaul at Aldenham following seven-year CoF expiry early in 1978, and a repaint in May 1980 explains why it looks smart here.

*Opposite below:* **On 10** July 1980, Alexandra Palace was gutted by a disastrous fire for the second time in its 106-year history. According to local legend, gypsies who were evicted from their encampment at the top of Muswell Hill so that the palace could be built there put a curse on the building, predicting it would be burnt down three times. The first fire took place within a year of its opening, the third has yet to occur at the time of writing. Whatever the truth of this, the building was unsafe for several weeks afterwards, and route W3 'which serves it' had to be diverted away. On 12 July, however, the driver of Wood Green DMS916 has forgotten the diversion, and has to do a three-point turn in Station Road, Wood Green to reach it. The bus is also very unusually curtailed at Crouch End. This DMS was new in the autumn of 1974, replacing MBSs on Wood Green's W-series flat fare routes and remained there until withdrawal in May 1981. It saw further use in Hong Kong.

KING EDWARD
PANATELLAS
Waltham Cross
Great Cambridge Road
Westbury Avenue
217
ENFIELD
John Player Special KING SIZE
PLEASE PAY AS YOU ENTER
EGP 38J

White Hart Lane
Wood Grn Alexandra Pk
Ferme Park Road
W3
CROUCH END
TOTTENHAM LANE
Rothmans King Size
20p
SMU 916 N

*Above*: **The W3's** diversion was from Wood Green Underground Station along the High Road to Turnpike Lane Station, and then along route 144 as far as Priory Park in Hornsey, where it regained the correct line of route. Also on 12 July 1980, DMS899 passes beneath the bridge carrying Wood Green Shopping City across the High Road. Of note is its improvised via blind display. This DMS also spent its entire career on these routes, from September 1974 to August 1981 when displaced by new Metrobuses. However, it then went for scrap after over a year in store.

*Opposite above*: **Also of** the same batch, DMS910 heads along the High Road in the other direction, on the now superfluous route W4 which was entirely duplicated by the 29 and 123 between Turnpike Lane and Winchmore Hill (following March 1977 route revisions) and finally withdrawn at the end of September 1980. Having also been at Wood Green since new in September 1974, it was transferred to Edmonton as a result, until withdrawn after seven-year CoF expiry. It too never ran again, going for scrap after some two years in store.

*Opposite below*: **Next day,** 13 July 1980, DMS631 looks very smart in London Country NBC corporate light green and white livery when displayed at a special event in Crawley marking sixty years of the Green Line coach network. It is one of a handful that LCBS acquired in June for training duties, after it had spent its entire seven-year CoF period from new at Merton Garage. It spent a couple of years so employed, before being transferred within the NBC to Midland Red, who returned it to passenger service. The others did the same, some seeing service with subsequent operators well into the 1990s.

Wood Green High Rd
Palmers Green
Green Lanes
W4
WINCHMORE HILL
20p
SMU 910N

I'm a Bus-Drive me Earn good money up front
WE NEED DRIVERS NOW
CAUTION DRIVER UNDER INSTRUCTION
LONDON COUNTRY
DMS 631
MLK 631L

*Above*: **An oddity** at this period was DMS780, which was used at Edmonton Garage for some months as a crew-operated bus on route 279. On 19 July 1980, it pulls out of Edmonton Green Bus Station with an RM following. By accident or design, it had also worked as a crew bus on route 16 when new for a few months. Withdrawn upon initial seven-year CoF expiry the following November, it saw further use in Hong Kong.

*Opposite above*: **The summer** of 1980 saw a continued shrinking of DM/DMS territory north of the Thames, with Metrobuses invading from the west, and Titans from the east. On 22 July, Finchley DMS127 turns from Chase Side, Southgate into Osidge Lane. Having been overhauled to that garage in the autumn of 1978, it later moved to Willesden, only to return in June 1980 after expulsion from there by Metrobuses. They also replaced it at Finchley when they caught up with it there in November. Having spent a couple of months at Camberwell, it ended up at Uxbridge where it was finally withdrawn in August 1981, going for scrap eventually thereafter.

*Opposite below*: **For many** years, it was standard practice for London Transport to keep some of their older, withdrawn buses for use as driver trainers or for staff transport. This is still so with their successors today. However, a new departure in the late 1970s/early 1980s was to use COF-expired DMSs, all of seven years old or less, as trainers. RMs and RMLs that had latterly been so used were returned to service to help get rid of DMs and DMSs. On 23 July 1980, DMS1420 takes a break at Holloway, Nag's Head. It had managed some six years and nine months' service at various South London garages before demotion - and survived as a trainer until the summer of 1992.

125
NORTH FINCHLEY
A MOVING EXHIBITION
We're with the Woolwich!
ZONE
PLEASE PAY AS YOU ENTER
EGP 127J

How can you save money on bus fares?
PRIVATE
Pass.
BUS STOP
SERVICE
TEXACO
PLEASE PAY AS YOU ENTER
MLH 420L

*Above*: **On 24** July 1980, Edmonton DM1115 arrives at Lower Edmonton Station (later renamed Edmonton Green, in accordance with the shopping centre and bus station across the road from it) on long-forgotten route 283. This was introduced using crew DMs at the end of October 1978, and withdrawn less than two years later at the end of September 1980. It was an attempt at localising the outer section of the long route 279, taking over its routeing between Hammond Street and Waltham Cross, and overlapping it as far as Edmonton Green. It was not a success, perhaps because of the unreliability of the DMs – more than once, RMs from route 279's allocation had to sub for nearly all of its allocation of them. The 279 was thus re-extended out to Hammond Street, using RMs and RCLs. This DM only ever worked from Edmonton Garage, from new in July 1975 to withdrawal in May 1982, latterly suffering the ignominy of being spare cover for the Routemasters on routes 149 and 279. It never ran again.

*Opposite above*: **Damage to** Alexandra Palace after the fire was so severe that normal service was not resumed on route W3 until September. In the meantime, to avoid confusion with route W2 which also linked Finsbury Park with Crouch End and Hornsey, they ran on their diversion with blank via blinds. On 20 July 1980, Wood Green DMS889 has just turned right from the High Road at Turnpike Lane Station as the point inspector looks on. It spent its entire LT working life at that garage, from September 1974 until February 1981, later being exported for further use in Hong Kong.

*Below*: **On 2** August 1980, Hanwell DMS1957 loads up in Ealing Road, Greenford on flat-fare route E2. New in November 1975 to this garage, where DMSs replaced the awful MBS 'cattle-trucks' on routes E1 and E2, it spent its entire LT career there, and after being ousted by new Metrobuses six years later and withdrawn, it was sold to Maidstone & District. It ran for a creditable ten years with that fleet, once again showing how DMSs seemed to be much more reliable with provincial fleets than they were in London. Even now, many people blame the LT maintenance regime of the 1970s and 1980s, geared to looking after RF, RM and RT-types, for their failure here.

***Above*: At Hanwell** Garage itself, DM1198 has developed a fault and has to be subbed, interrupting its passengers' journeys heading towards Uxbridge on the busy 207. The garage point inspector may be seen on the right, taking its running plates to put them on to a replacement DM waiting outside. The offending DM was also new to Hanwell, entering service in February 1976, replacing RMLs on the 207. That route's passengers would not have to put up with them for much longer, however, since the route reverted to RM/RML operation a couple of weeks after this incident, taking until Christmas to complete, and like the 16 and 16A featuring many ex-London Country RMLs. Exiled to Croydon, DM1198 perished amid the Law Lords' changes of September 1982 but saw further use in Hong Kong. DMS1960 'on the right' was another to be new here for the E1 and E2, moving to South London after displacement by Metrobuses. It had a light overhaul at Aldenham late in 1981 but was withdrawn two years later. Eventually, it saw a few years' use in the late 1980s/early 1990s with Metrobus of Orpington, running on contract operating London bus routes in that area.

***Opposite above*: On Sunday,** 10 August 1980, a very full Clapton DMS2232 crosses the Regent's Canal in Kingsland High Road, Haggerston on route 22A. Its passengers are probably heading for the famous Sunday morning street markets of Club Row and 'Petticoat Lane'. Amongst the last few Gardner-engined Metro-Cammell-bodied DMSs delivered (in May 1977) before the B20-type supplanted them, it had only recently been transferred to Clapton, and worked at a variety of garages until withdrawn when only six years old in May 1983. However, it went on to serve various provincial operators for more than twenty years. Route 22A had been introduced using new DMSs in October 1972, graduating to Titan operation in August 1982 when Clapton's DMS allocation was replaced by them.

*Below*: **More than** a month after the disastrous Alexandra Palace fire, route W3 was still unable to pass over the hill beside it through Alexandra Park. In the meantime, a free shuttle service was introduced connecting Wood Green Underground Station with the British Rail Great Northern suburban line station then named Wood Green (for Alexandra Park). On 12 August 1980, Wood Green DM1184 loads up at Spouters Corner opposite the tube station. Since no fares were collected, this normally crew-operated DM could work as an OPO vehicle. It had entered service at Wood Green, its only garage when with LT, replacing RMs on route 29 in December 1975, being switched to route 141 in March 1977. It too perished amid the September 1982 cuts, ending up in Hong Kong. Of note is the newly-overhauled former Green Line coach RCL following on route 243. These had just re-entered service, replacing DMs on route 149, but often subbed for RMs and RMLs on the 243/243A and 253 at Stamford Hill already.

*Above*: **Finchley DMS380** still looks quite smart after its November 1979 overhaul when passing County Gate, the former border between Hertfordshire and Middlesex on the Great North Road in Barnet on route 263, on 21 August 1980. It had entered service replacing RTs on route 44 in June 1972, working at various garages, until withdrawn in November 1981, then being stored for several months before going for scrap. It had been ousted from Finchley Garage by new Metrobuses in November 1980.

*Opposite above*: **Over in** South London, the very hilly route 192 in the Woolwich and Plumstead area was not a healthy environment for the troublesome DMSs. On 24 August 1980, New Cross DMS779 heads for home along Herbert Road, Plumstead. The route's normal northern terminus was Lewisham, but before London's bus fleets were privatised, it was normal practice for buses based at 'off-route' garages to run to and from them in service. New to Finchley Garage in November 1973, this DMS managed its full seven-year CoF span and was sold for further use in Hong Kong. Route 192 had been converted from RM to DMS operation in April 1978, receiving MDs at the end of October 1981 but withdrawn amid the September 1982 cuts.

*Opposite below*: **On** 31 August 1980, Walthamstow DMS1863 is unusually curtailed at Gants Hill Station rather than completing the 144's full route from Muswell Hill Broadway to Ilford Station. It collects passengers at the western end of Park Road, Hornsey. New in June 1975, it spent most of its life at this garage until ousted by new Titans in January 1982 and withdrawn. It was later used by Ensign as a London tourist bus.

Go wherever you want with a Red Bus Rover Ticket.
192
NEW CROSS GARAGE
Britain's best cars at competitive hire rates
TGX 779M
DGJ 500H
PMENT

144
GANTS HILL STATION
GHM 863N

*Above*: **Conversely, on** the same occasion DMS916 is almost empty when passing the ruined south east tower of Alexandra Palace. A pub had occupied its ground floor, and when the fire took hold, spirits stored beneath it in the basement exploded, blowing its roof off. Except for being ousted from Wood Green earlier, in May 1981, this DMS had the same history as the one in the previous picture.

*Opposite*: **On 2** September 1980, buses on route W3 are finally allowed to resume their correct routeing over the hill through Alexandra Park. Wood Green DMS874 collects a large number of passengers in Station Road, opposite Wood Green Underground Station. This is another that spent its entire London life at that garage, entering service to replace its MBSs in October 1974 and withdrawn when ousted by Metrobuses in August 1981. It is also another to end up in Hong Kong.

***Above*: Also in** my home area, Muswell Hill B20 DM2567 has been unusually curtailed at Palmers Green Garage when working their Sunday allocation of the 102 on 14 September 1980. It was one of those ousted by RMLs from the 16, having entered service in April 1978. After again being replaced by RMs and RMLs on routes 43 and 102 in September 1982, it was converted for OPO and spent the best part of ten years at various South London garages. Used by a number of private owners after sale, it ended up as a caravan on the South Coast.

***Opposite above*: On the** same day, Potters Bar DMS1901 approaches route 84's New Barnet Station terminus. This route was still SMS-operated at the time on Mondays to Saturdays, but converted daily to DMS a fortnight later. This one had been new in September 1975, replacing MBs on route 242, and received an Aldenham overhaul in the winter of 1981/82. Subsequently used at a number of South London garages, it was demoted in the mid-1980s to training duties after a long period in store. However, it was resurrected for the ill-fated, cheapskate Kingstonbus scheme in 1987 and withdrawn when that collapsed a couple of years later, used briefly as a trainer again and then scrapped.

***Opposite below*: Also that** day, Ponders End B20 DMS2405 sets off from Oakwood Station on route 217B's Sunday extension there from Enfield Town. This route had been the last route to be newly introduced with RTs, as late as April 1976. It converted to new B20 DMSs, including this one, in August 1977 along with parent route 217. Ousted by new Metrobuses early in 1982, it then had an Aldenham overhaul, spending the best part of ten years at various South London garages before withdrawal. It then had a similar length of time with various independent fleets before going for scrap.

TAYLOR & MELHUISH
VERNONS
KING EDWARD
84
NEW BARNET STATION
KUC 901P

UNDERGROUND
217B
OJD 405R

***Above*: A visit** to Aldenham Works itself on 18 September 1980 finds the gutted remains of DMS216. This unfortunate vehicle had entered service at Thornton Heath Garage replacing RMs on route 64 in December 1971, remaining there until overhaul almost seven years later. Initially sent to Peckham, it moved to Catford Garage after replacement by MDs on route 78 in February 1980. Has it fallen victim to a cigarette end in its front upper-deck seats, when ironically advertising such things? Not surprisingly, it was scrapped as a result.

*Above*: **A third** damaged DMS at Aldenham that day is DMS2172. It has lost its front upper-deck windows, also apparently as a result of fire damage at Catford Garage. Despite being less than four years old, and not seemingly too badly damaged, it was also withdrawn. However, its chassis was kept for a few years as an instruction unit. The vehicle had briefly worked from Elmers End Garage, before moving to Catford in February 1977 to replace RTs on route 75.

*Opposite below*: **Also at** Aldenham that day, DMS388 has an even more badly burnt-out front upper deck. It had entered service at Wandsworth Garage on route 44 in June 1972, moved briefly to Merton before overhaul in the autumn of 1979, also ending up at Catford. The fact it suffered a similar fate to DMS216 suggests either arson or the possibility that one set the other on fire in the garage. At any rate, it too was scrapped as a result. In the foreground, Metrobus M202 and RML2444 have suffered front-end damage, and await repairs.

***Above*: On the** same day, Edgware DMS2145 collects passengers in Manor Way, Borehamwood in the evening rush hour. Its destination 'Edgware ABC Cinema' shows it is running in to its garage, perhaps a result of a staff cut. It had entered service at Romford, North Street Garage in November 1976, being replaced there three years later by new Titans. Having been at Catford in the meantime, it arrived at Edgware in July 1980, replacing CoF-expired DMSs new to the 292 seven years earlier, only to be displaced by new Metrobuses in January 1981 and sent south again to Merton. It was another victim of the Law Lords in September 1982, but survived to see further service in Hong Kong into the 1990s.

***Opposite above*: Also in** that evening rush hour, Ponders End B20 DMS2460 shares the 231's terminus at Carterhatch with RM450 on route 135, which will convert to DMS nine days later. By now, all DMSs at the garage had been replaced by B20s. This one had been new in July 1977 for the 217/217B conversion the following month, route 231 having initially converted from RT to SMS operation in the autumn of 1971. Expelled by new Metrobuses in early 1982, and given an Aldenham overhaul, it was resettled south of the river, ending up at Stockwell for several years before being withdrawn and sold for scrap in March 1991.

***Opposite below*: By this** time, Palmers Green Garage's allocation of DMSs had been replaced by the newer B20 type, too. On 20 September 1980, DMS2479 heads south along East Barnet Road on route 261, which will be withdrawn a week later and replaced by alterations to routes 26 and 84. The DMS had also been new in the summer of 1977, being used on the Round London Sightseeing Tour from Stockwell Garage until moved north in the summer of 1978, a couple of months after the 261's conversion to the type from RM. Upon replacement by Metrobuses at Palmers Green early in 1982, it was overhauled that May and sent to Shepherd's Bush Garage, only to be displaced by them again there eighteen months later. It too ended up in South London, being finally withdrawn from Sutton Garage in the spring of 1992, and also scrapped a few months later.

KING EDWARD
231
CARTERHATCH
KING EDWARD
135
OJD460R

Meadway New Barnet
Church Hill Road
Hampden Way
261
ARNOS GROVE STN
A MOVING EXHIBITION
THX 479S

*Above*: **On the** same day as the previous picture, Potters Bar DMS1880 is at the junction of Cockfosters Road and Bramley Road working route 299, which was normally SMS-operated on Mondays to Saturdays at this time and withdrawn a week later. Route 299 has since been reintroduced serving this area, as it still does today. The DMS had been new to Potters Bar, replacing MBs, in August 1975, receiving an Aldenham overhaul six years later and sent south to Merton. However, it lasted less than two years there, being one of the hundreds sold to Ensign Bus and seeing little PSV use afterwards.

*Opposite above*: **Also on** 20 September 1980, Edmonton DM1815 departs from its home garage at the end of Tramway Avenue to rattle its way to Liverpool Street on route 149. By now, Stamford Hill's allocation of newly-overhauled RCLs to replace these contraptions had been completed, and Edmonton was beginning to receive theirs but it took until December to receive them all. This DM had entered service replacing RTs at Brixton in March 1975, and only arrived at Edmonton in November 1979. It would be expelled by RCLs a week after I took this picture, and moved to Loughton to work on OPO services. It was yet another to perish as a result of the 1982 route cuts, never to run again.

*Opposite below*: **Route 168A,** operated by Holloway, was one of those converted to crew DM in January 1975, replacing RTs. The route was never scheduled for Routemasters operation, but the unreliability of the DMs meant they often had to sub for them. RMs often did so, but the use of RMLs was very rare. On 6 October 1980, however, RML2696 has had to be fielded, passing DM1082 on the route's Hornsey Rise stand. The DM had been new to Holloway for the RT to DM conversion of route 4 in June 1975, being banished by RM conversion of that route and the 172 in the spring of 1981 to Thornton Heath for the 109. However, it was yet another to perish amid the Law Lords' cuts when replaced there by RMs, and after a long time in store went for scrap early in 1984. The 1967-registered RML lasted until the first decade of the present century.

EDMONTON GARAGE
VALLIER
149
LIVERPOOL STREET
GHM 815N

168A
Kings Cross
Farringdon Road
Fleet Street
CLAPHAM JUNCTION
save money on bus fares?
Pass
SMK 696
Caledonian Road
Kings+ Blackfriars
Waterloo Vauxhall
168A
HORNSEY RISE
GHV 82 N

*Above*: **By the** end of 1980, surviving DMs were being equipped for dual crew/OPO use, and fitted with a flap below the windscreen saying 'Pay Conductor' or 'Pay Driver', as appropriate. They were reclassified plain 'D' as a result. On Christmas Eve 1980, Stockwell D2611 apparently has no relief crew when waiting in Bondway, Vauxhall (are they prematurely celebrating Christmas in the nearby Royal Vauxhall Tavern?) and passengers have been transferred to the one behind. It had been new to the garage for the RLST in June 1978, later working the 168. Overhauled in the spring of 1982, it was outshopped to Brixton Garage, later returning to Stockwell from where it was withdrawn early in 1991, being scrapped soon thereafter.

*Opposite above*: **On New** Year's Day 1981, Walthamstow DMS1843 is at Chingford Mount on circular route W21, which had been introduced with MBSs upon 'Reshaping' in September 1968. The vehicle had been new to replace them there in June 1975, being withdrawn in the summer of 1981 following ousting by new Titans. It saw several years' use with independent operators after a couple of years in store and eventual sale. The W21, meanwhile, was withdrawn a month after I took this picture, replaced by new routes 97A and 212, which this DMS worked until withdrawal.

*Opposite below*: **Also that** day, winter sunshine catches Leyton DMS2183 as it sets off from route 55's Walthamstow Garage terminus for Aldwych. The route was reverted to crew operation using RMs at the end of the month, having been converted from RT to DMS in October 1972. Having entered service in December 1976, this one moved to Leyton in September 1979, and by coincidence was transferred to Walthamstow as a result of the 55's loss of the type. However, it was withdrawn in January 1982, later seeing further service in Hong Kong.

WALTHAMSTOW CIRCULAR
W21
VIA PROSPECT HILL
GHM 843N
G&H

TRAMWAY
55
ALDWYCH
PLEASE PAY AS YOU ENTER
OJD 183R

*Above*: **Still showing** the fleet number DM2582, this B20 example was an early conversion from crew to crew/OPO mode, being one of those transferred from Cricklewood to Muswell Hill Garage upon the RML conversion of routes 16 and 16A when just over two years old in May 1980. On 6 January 1981, it loads up on route W7 outside Hornsey Town Hall in Crouch End Broadway. Resettled in South London after replacement by Metrobuses in February 1982, it ended up at Thornton Heath Garage until being withdrawn in the spring of 1992, seeing brief use with Midland Fox before scrapping in 1995.

*Opposite above*: **Changes to** route 23 in April 1981 saw it extended westwards, overlapping the 15 as far as Ladbroke Grove, and also reverted to crew operation on Sundays, putting paid to DMS OPO use that day. Easter Monday, 20 April, was their penultimate day, on which Upton Park DMS1931 heads east at Gardiners Corner, Aldgate, scene of the notorious riots in 1936. This DMS spent most of its working life at that garage, being new in October 1975, and overhauled six years later after displacement by new Titans. It was, however, withdrawn in the summer of 1983 and also ended up with Midland Fox after sale.

*Opposite below*: **On 23** April 1981, Putney DMS2243 calls at Putney Heath, Green Man on local route 85A, four days before the route was withdrawn and replaced by alterations to route 170. New in June 1977, the DMS was one of the last non-B20 examples built, and was transferred to Putney in October 1979. It was however withdrawn in May 1983 and, after a considerable time in store, sold for further service with a variety of operators (including Metrobus on LRT-contracted services) until the late 1990s.

From A to B...
Limehouse Poplar Canning Town East Ham Barking
23
BECONTREE HEATH
...to C to D to...
ISHERWOOD
BARCLAYS BANK
PLEASE PAY AS YOU ENTER
KUC931P
MOST FAMOUS KOSHER RESTAURANT IN

GREEN MAN
From A to B...
PUTNEY BRIDGE STN & DANEBURY AVENUE
85A
...to C to D to...
KING SIZE
PUTNEY HEATH
PLEASE PAY AS YOU ENTER
Flat Fare Bus
OJD 243R

*Above*: **Further south** that day, Thornton Heath DMS277 is at Hackbridge Corner on the last leg of the very circuitous route 115 (also withdrawn four days later), which ran what should have been a short distance from Wallington to Purley all the way around, as the DMS's blind says, via Hackbridge, Mitcham, Streatham and Norbury. This DMS spent almost the whole of its initial seven-year CoF span at New Cross, after entering service to replace RTs on route 177 in January 1972. Overhauled at Aldenham early in 1979, and sent to Thornton Heath, it was however withdrawn in June 1982, languishing in store unwanted until going for scrap two years later.

*Opposite above*: **On 2** May 1981, DMSs have been shuddering and rattling their way between Moorgate and Highgate Village on route 271 for over ten years. However, increasing maintenance problems by now meant that, sometimes, LS class single-deckers at Holloway Garage for routes 210 and 239 had to sub for them. Thus the very rare spectacle of a single- and double-deck vehicle together on the same LT Central Area route is seen at Moorgate, Finsbury Square as LS174 sets off leaving DMS385 on the stand: a far cry from the graceful trolleybuses on route 611 which the 271 replaced in July 1960. The DMS had entered service at Wandsworth, replacing RTs on route 44 in June 1972, moving to Putney in January 1979. It was overhauled and sent to Holloway in the summer of that year, but withdrawn three years later, never to run again.

*Opposite below*: **Upton Park** DMS1931, which we saw working their Sunday allocation on route 23 a couple of weeks earlier, now finds itself on route 5 in East Ham High Street South on 7 May 1981, turning short at the nearby White Horse terminus with blinds already set for the return to Aldgate. Most oddly, it is subbing for a Routemasters and working as a crew vehicle, despite this route having reverted from DMS OPO to RM/RML crew operation a couple of weeks previously, after ten unhappy years of DMSs.

271
THX 174S
JUST BORED?
temp with
Kelly Girl
Holloway Road
Caledonian Road
Old Street Station
271
MOORGATE
BETWEEN JOBS?
temp with
Kelly Girl
JGF 385K

From A to B...
Bloomsbury Old St
Aldgate Poplar
East Ham Barking
5
ALDGATE
...to C to D to...
EAST HAM COLLEGE OF TECHNOLOGY
PLEASE PAY AS YOU ENTER
KUC931P

***Above: A little*** further south that day, also approaching the terminus, DMS2134 is another Upton Park vehicle, on route 147. DMSs had, as so often on outer London routes, replaced SMSs on this one. This vehicle had entered service at Ponders End in October 1976, replacing SMSs on route 231, being displaced there the following July by new B20 DMSs and transferred to Upton Park. It remained there until being displaced again, this time by Titans, in June 1982 and moved to Camberwell but was withdrawn two months later. It was eventually sold for further use in Hong Kong.

***Opposite above: Another Upton*** Park bus caught by my camera on 7 May 1981 is DMS1925, in London Road approaching Barking town centre on route 238, yet another on which they replaced SMSs. It entered service in November 1975, briefly at Ponders End, then moving after a few days to Upton Park where it remained until Aldenham overhaul in the summer of 1981. Outshopped to Catford in October that year, it was however withdrawn in September 1983, and is yet another to go for scrap after a long period in store, unwanted by anyone.

***Opposite below: The short*** North London suburban route 244, which ran from Southgate Station via Bounds Green to Muswell Hill, with a rush hour extension to Golders Green paralleling the 102, had a variety of OPO types working it in its final year of operation. On 15 May 1981, Muswell Hill D2577 approaches its terminus in that town's Broadway. This is another that had been expelled from Cricklewood by RML conversion of the 16 and 16A when only two years old a year previously. After overhaul in February 1982, it migrated south of the Thames, working at various garages and ending up at Stockwell. It went for scrap a few months after November 1990 withdrawal.

John Player Special
KING SIZE
Upton Park
East Ham Barking
Goodmayes
238
LITTLE HEATH
PLEASE PAY AS YOU ENTER
KUC 925P

BARCLAY
Powys Lane
Bounds Green Station
Alexandra Park Road
244
MUSWELL HILL BDY
John Player Special KING SIZE
ackmans
THX577 S

*Above*: **In the** far west of London, DMSs were well on their way out by this time, too. Uxbridge DMS116 loads up in Vine Street, in its home town, on route 223, which previously had drastically been upgraded from RF to operation by them, on 1 June 1981. It was the penultimate member of the first batch of DMSs, having entered service on route 5 in April 1971. Overhauled in September 1978, it was withdrawn in August 1981, never to run again. Metrobuses replaced them at Uxbridge.

*Opposite above*: **Newer examples** fared little better, once LT had given up the ghost with them. On 3 June 1981, a very smart Potters Bar DMS2245 is at Southgate Station heading south on route 298. New in July 1977 to Seven Kings Garage for RT replacement on route 148, it was ousted from there by Titans in July 1980, moving to Finchley as a result. But only four months later, Metrobuses replaced it there, so it moved north to Potters Bar. They caught up with it there too in April 1982, whereupon it was sent to Sutton Garage. The following September saw it shunted across to South Croydon amid the service cuts, only to be withdrawn just two months later after only five years and four months' LT service, having been the penultimate non-B20 DMS. After sale, it survived until 1995 with various new operators.

*Opposite below*: **The years** 1981 and 1982 saw the replacement of most of the remaining crew-operated DMs by Routemasters. On 10 June 1981, a well-filled Camberwell DM1067 passes County Hall, headquarters of LT's GLC overlords who helped speed the DMs and DMSs on their way, on route 172, turning short at Bloomsbury. The route had received them to replace RTs at the end of August 1975, but was now RM-operated with DMs acting as spares for them. Withdrawn as seven-year CoF expiry approached in June 1982, this one saw further use with various operators until as late as 2008.

FARE DEAL 25p.
Palmers Grn Southgate
Chase Side Cockfosters
Potters Bar Mutton Lane
298
TURNPIKE LANE STN
Any bus ride. Anywhere in the Flat Fare Area.
FARE DEAL
25p.
PLEASE PAY AS YOU ENTER
OJD 245R

Barnsbury Angel
Charing + Westminster
Kennington Brixton
172
BLOOMSBURY
GHV 67N
From A to B..
12
EAST ACTON
..to C to D to
395 CLT

*Above*: **Looking very** smart on 20 June 1981, Palmers Green DMS2330 heads along Silver Street in Upper Edmonton bound for Whipps Cross on route 34. This one had entered service at Wandsworth (replacing earlier examples) in January 1978, but was delicensed just three months later, spending a very long time off the road. It was eventually resurrected at Palmers Green Garage in May 1981, only to be sent to Aldenham for overhaul in March 1982. Outshopped to Merton in June, it remained there until withdrawal in July 1990, going for scrap thereafter.

*Opposite above*: **On 23** June 1981, Edmonton DMS1498 departs from Chase Farm Hospital on route W8. This had been renumbered from 128 in the summer of 1969 and DMSs had subsequently replaced its original MBSs. This one had been new to replace RTs at Clapton on route 277 in January 1974, and was one of a number of DMSs given three-year recertifications, rather than overhauls, to keep them going after initial seven-year CoF expiry until suitable replacements could be procured. Done only in October 1980, it was withdrawn in July 1982 following replacement by Metrobuses and never ran again.

*Opposite below*: **Having worked** the inner section of route 221 (which had replaced trolleybus routes 521 and 621) from Holborn, Wood Green DMS1621 arrives at North Finchley on 23 June 1981. The route had converted from RM to this type in March 1973, and this one had been new to Barking Garage in February 1974. Expelled from there by Titans in July 1980 and sent to Sutton, it was overhauled to Wood Green in March 1981, and still looks smart in this picture. Ousted from there by Metrobuses in November that year, it moved to Merton and then Thornton Heath, being withdrawn in December 1983 and ending up at Hendon Metropolitan Police College.

NEW NESCAFÉ-
Richer smoother
NESCAFÉ
NEW IMPROVED ROAST
Lower Edmonton
Enfield Town
Lavender Hill
W8
LOWER EDMONTON STN
DMS 1498
PLEASE PAY AS YOU ENTER
MLH 498L

FARE DEAL 25p.
221
NORTH FINCHLEY
Any bus ride. Anywhere in the Flat Fare Area.
FALMERS
PLEASE PAY AS YOU ENTER
THM 621M

*Above*: **At Stonebridge** Park Garage on 28 June 1981, DMS321 and DMS1967 accompany two Metrobuses on route 18, where they have recently replaced crew DMs. The 112 had been converted from RT to SMS in May 1971, receiving DMSs some six years later. DMS321 had been new to Peckham Garage for route 78 in April 1972, being overhauled to Stonebridge Park in August 1979. It was withdrawn two years later when the garage closed, seeing a couple of years' service with other operators thereafter. DMS1967, meanwhile, had entered service at Cricklewood in January 1976, moving to Finchley in February 1978, being displaced by Metrobuses there two years later and sent to Stonebridge Park. After that garage's closure, it was transferred to Merton, from where it was demoted to training duties at the end of 1983. Finally retired by LT in January 1992, it spent some ten years with various owners as a non-PSV before being exported to the Continent.

*Opposite above*: **Less than** seven years after they replaced the ill-fated MBSs on Wood Green flat-fare routes W2 and W3 (as well as the W1 and W4, later withdrawn), DMS876 and DMS909 are themselves threatened with replacement by new Metrobuses, one of which is behind them on the stand at Alexandra Park, Victoria Stakes on 29 June 1981. Both have worked short journeys of their respective routes in the evening rush hour. Both had entered service in October 1974, spending their entire LT lives at Wood Green until withdrawal in August 1981. DMS876 never ran again, but DMS909 saw further service in Hong Kong.

*Opposite below*: **Trolleybus replacement** route 259 converted from RM to DMS operation in February 1973. On 2 July 1981, Edmonton DMS2234 has just set off from its Holborn Circus terminus on a trip to its home garage. It had entered service in July 1977 at Southall Garage, being replaced there by Metrobuses in September 1979 and sent to Leyton. Here, it was displaced by route 55 being converted from DMS OPO to RM crew operation and moved to Edmonton, replacing earlier time-expired DMSs at the end of January 1981. Ousted from there by new Metrobuses in July 1982, it moved to Battersea, where it perished a few weeks later in the September cuts. It therefore saw just over five years' LT service. However, it saw use with various other operators until 2001.

How can you save money on bus fares?
W3
FINSBURY PARK STN
Pass
From A to B...
W2
...to C to D to...
PLEASE PAY AS YOU ENTER
SMU 909 N
TGX 876 M

Tottenham
Finsbury Park
Caledonian Road
259
EDMONTON
The greatest name in King Size
PLEASE PAY AS YOU ENTER
OJD 234R
BUS STOP

***Above*: On the** same route, but working from Tottenham Garage, early DMS16 shudders its way north along Fore Street, Upper Edmonton on 4 July 1981. One of the first DMSs to enter service, at Shepherd's Bush on route 220 at the beginning of January 1971, it remained there until Aldenham overhaul, from which it emerged in April 1978. It perished in June 1982, replaced by new Metrobuses, never to run again and ending up providing spares for the well-known independent operator Stevenson of Spath.

***Opposite above*: With the** burnt-out wreck of the allegedly cursed Alexandra Palace atop Muswell Hill in the background, a very full Wood Green DMS876 pollutes the rarefied atmosphere of the Northern Heights as it climbs steep Ferme Park Road through Crouch End on 7 July 1981. As related earlier, the days of this Wood Green DMS were now very much numbered.

***Opposite below*: Route 121** had begun life as a short route linking Enfield and Chingford across the Lea Valley, but in September 1980 was extended west from Enfield to Oakwood, and on from that point to Turnpike Lane, replacing route 298A. On 23 July 1981, Ponders End DMS2463 is unusually curtailed at Enfield Town from the south when calling at Southgate Station. This B20 DMS had entered service at Palmers Green replacing RTs on route 34 in September 1977, being later moved up the road to Ponders End where the type ousted older DMSs. Upon replacement by new Metrobuses in February 1982, it went for overhaul at Aldenham, being banished to Brixton Garage when outshopped in May. It then survived in use in South London until July 1992, seeing use after sale with a variety of operators until the late 1990s.

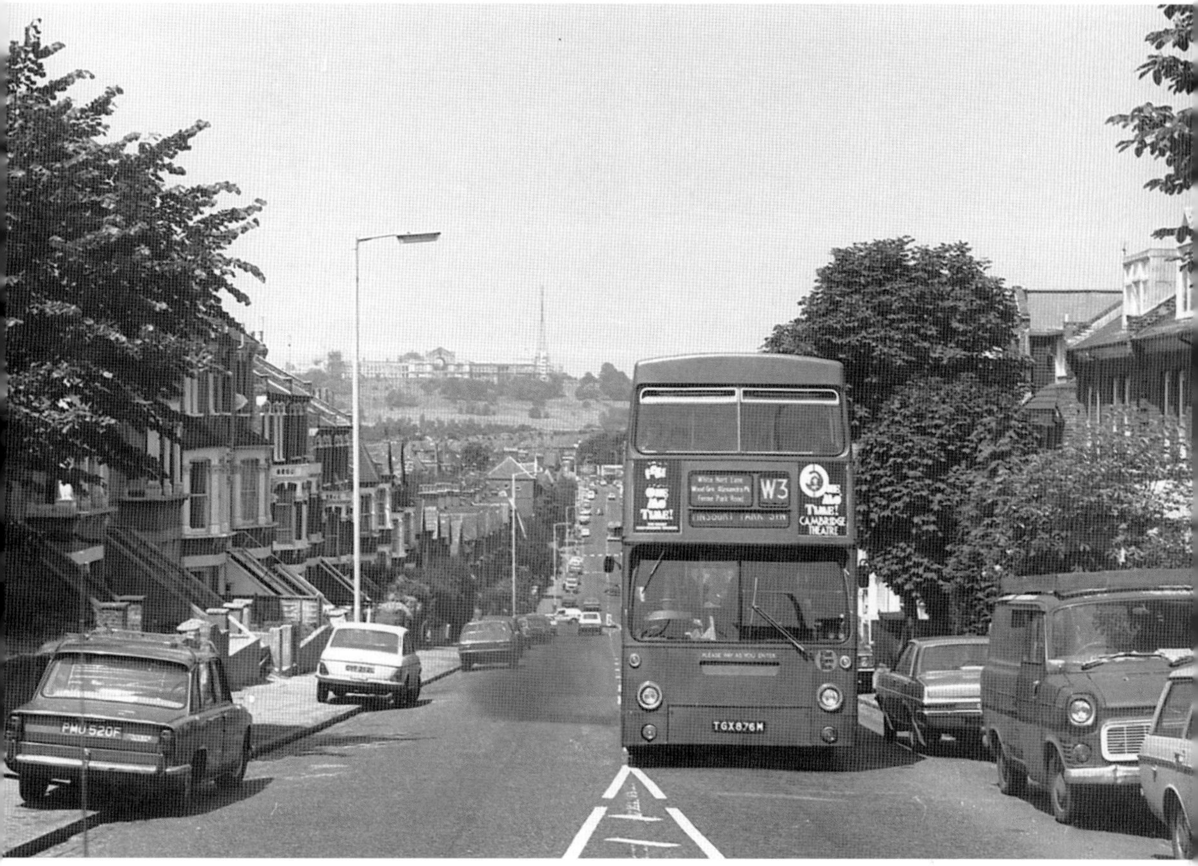
W3
CAMBRIDGE THEATRE
PMU 520F
TGX876M

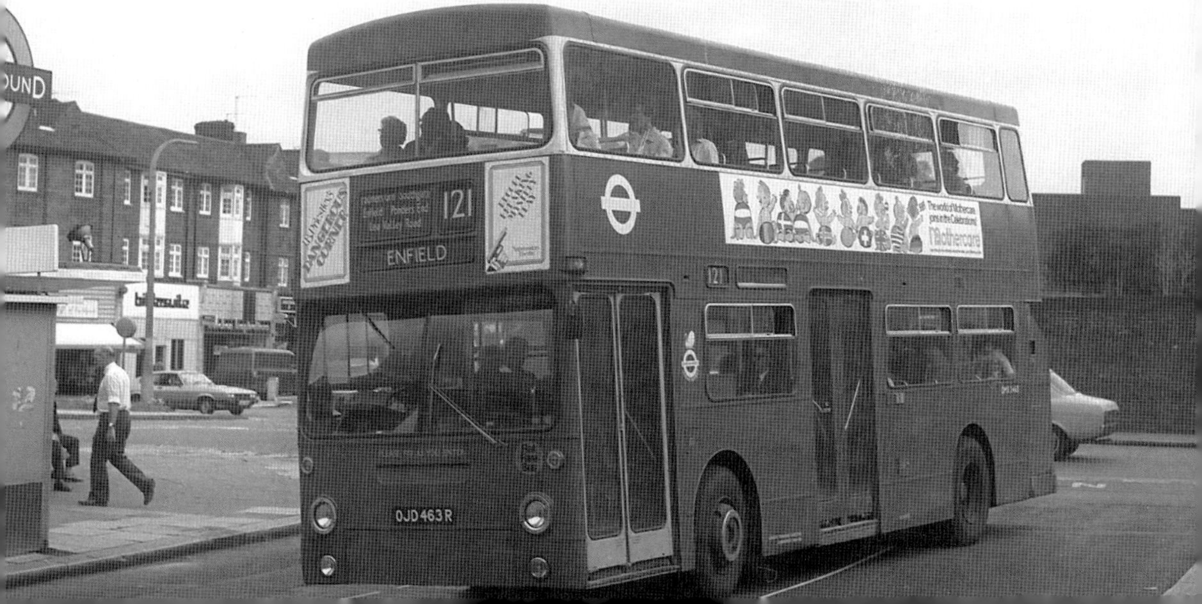
121
ENFIELD
OJD463R

*Above*: **On 14** August 1981, at Palmers Green Garage itself, DMS2453 runs in off route 34, perhaps owing to a staff cut. It too had been new to the route in September 1977, going to Aldenham for overhaul in October 1981, emerging four months later to Bexleyheath Garage. Transferred in March 1983 to South Croydon, it spent just over ten years, latterly as a trainer, in South West London until disposal in May 1993, after which it was scrapped.

*Opposite above*: **On the** same day as the previous picture, Stonebridge Park DMS1974 has just set off from Palmers Green Garage and waits to turn right onto the North Circular Road to begin its long trek around it to Ealing. It had been new to Stonebridge Park replacing SMSs on route 112 in May 1976, and this was its last day in LT service. However, it was sold for further use with Stevenson of Spath, lasting there until late 1990. Sister vehicle DMS1973 in the previous picture had exactly the same fate, lasting a few months longer with Stevenson's.

*Opposite below*: **On 17** August 1981, Walthamstow DMS105 is unusually curtailed at Seven Sisters Corner (previously known as Ward's Corner) when running along Broad Lane, Tottenham on trolleybus replacement route 123. DMSs had replaced RMs on this in March 1977. This one had been new to West Ham for the similar conversion of route 5 in April 1971, and been overhauled in July 1978. It had always been in the East, being transferred to Walthamstow in May 1981 and withdrawn upon replacement by new Titans the following November, never to run again.

ONE MO TIME!
112
EALING BROADWAY
ONE MO TIME! CAMBRIDGE THEATRE
Grants
KUC 974P

LION OF THE DESERT
LEICESTER SQ. THEATRE
From August 27
BOOK NOW!
123
SEVEN SISTERS CORNER
FARE DEAL
25p.
COOPER
49
EGP 105J

*Above*: **An unusual** working on 24 August 1981 is that of Shepherd's Bush B20 D2540, at Elephant & Castle in crew mode subbing for an RM on route 12. It had been new to Brixton in February 1978, later moving to Wandsworth and then in December 1980 for the RM to DMS conversion of route 72 at Shepherd's Bush. Transferred to Holloway in August 1983 upon displacement by Metrobuses, it would end up back in South West London, in common with most B20s. After a year's use as a trainer, it was retired in January 1992, being scrapped thereafter.

*Opposite above*: **At this** time, whereas Brixton Garage's share of the busy 109 had reverted from crew DM to RM operation in August 1981, the Thornton Heath share remained DM until the Law Lords' cuts of September 1982 released sufficient RMs to convert its share, too. In addition, many crews preferred the doored vehicles owing to assaults and muggings of conductors when passing through downtown Brixton. A year beforehand, on 2 September 1981, their DM1077 has just called at Kennington Church. It had been new to Stockwell Garage six years previously for the RT to DM conversion of the 168, moving to Thornton Heath (to replace RMs on the 109) three years after that. Upon their return on 4 September 1982, it was withdrawn, never to run again. After languishing in store, it suffered the ignominy of being wrecked at Chiswick Works in July 1983 when being repeatedly used as a 'turnover vehicle' during an open weekend to celebrate LT's Golden Jubilee.

*Opposite below*: **Foreshadowing the** allocation of 'production' examples there, prototype B20 DMS854 was allocated to Catford Garage in July 1980, having entered service at Chalk Farm in April 1974, moving to Cricklewood the same month until displacement by Metrobuses. On 2 September 1981, it approaches Eltham Church working route 124. Withdrawn two years later, it was exported to Hong Kong.

FARE DEAL 25p.
Kennington Brixton Streatham Norbury London Rd. Croydon
109
SOUTH CROYDON GARAGE
Any bus ride. Anywhere in the Flat Fare Area.
UJAMAA CENTRE
SILK CUT
DYNO ROD
GHV 77N

Falconwood Eltham Mottingham Grove Pk Catford Perry Vale
124
CATFORD
HAWES
PLEASE PAY AS YOU ENTER
TGX 854M

**The closure** of Stonebridge Park Garage saw route 18 actually revert for a while from Metrobus (which had replaced them there in June 1980) to crew DM operation. On 5 September 1981, in the heart of the area where crews demanded doored vehicles owing to conductors being mugged for their takings, Harlesden, DM2553 heads along Manor Road on the one-way system. Its destination, *Prince Of Wales* Harrow Road, suggests it is a staff cut, and running in to the new Westbourne Park Garage opened three weeks previously to replace Middle Row and Stonebridge Park garages. This DM had entered service in March 1978 replacing route 133's earlier DMs at Brixton, being ousted by RMs in August 1981. It moved to Thornton Heath in April 1983 upon replacement by Metrobuses on route 18, which was completed the following August, and was withdrawn in March 1992. It saw further service with Midland Fox and then non-PSV use.

**During their** time at Westbourne Park Garage, B20 DMs occasionally subbed for RMs on route 7. Also on 5 September 1981, DM2579 turns from Chepstow Road into Westbourne Grove. This had also come from Brixton, where it was new in March 1978 for the 133, moving to South Croydon upon replacement by Metrobuses in May 1983. However, it moved north again to Chalk Farm three months later, prior to returning to South West London in November 1984. Withdrawn in February 1991, it ended up with well-known independent operator Mayne of Manchester, lasting until 1997.

**On 6** October 1981, Walthamstow DMS1467 crosses the bridge over the long closed and lifted former Great Eastern Railway Palace Gates branch in Westbury Avenue, Wood Green. This DMS had been new in August 1973, not entering service until January 1974, at Clapton, replacing RTs on route 277. It is another to have been given a three-year recertification upon seven-year CoF expiry in August 1980, when it was sent to Walthamstow. Ousted by new Titans there, it was prematurely withdrawn in December 1981. However it saw further use in this area first with Crouch End Coaches and then as a school bus for Parnes House rabbinical college in Finchley. It later became a London sightseeing bus with London Pride, lasting until late 1993.

**Above: On 13** October 1981, DMS654, another of those sold to London Country for training, crosses the River Ravensbrook as a British Rail Class 47 diesel crosses the bridge with a freight into Lewisham Station. The DMS had entered service at Hornchurch Garage on route 165 in June 1973, being displaced by new Titans and sent to Catford in February 1979, and thus also working LT routes in Lewisham. It was withdrawn in May 1980 upon seven-year CoF expiry, passing to LCBS in June. It later saw further passenger use with Midland Red East and then Midland Fox from late 1982.

**Opposite: Also at** Lewisham that day, New Cross DMS1989 lays over in the bus station on the short route 151, which had been introduced in November 1972 with RTs to serve the new Ferrier Estate in Kidbrooke. RMs took over in the spring of 1975, then DMSs three years later. This one had entered service at Elmers End in June 1976, and had an overhaul back to New Cross in February 1982, only to be withdrawn two years later. It then saw further use with various operators until the late 1990s.

*Above*: **Passing Charlton** Station in the evening rush hour of the same day, DMS178 is also a New Cross vehicle, and heads home. It had been new to Bexleyheath Garage for the 96 in November 1971, the 177 did not receive them until two months later. In both cases they replaced RTs. This one was overhauled in January 1979, but perished in the changes of 4 September 1982. It saw further use as a non-PSV into the 1990s.

*Opposite*: **Back in** my home area, Muswell Hill B20 D2593 – one of the first conversions to hybrid crew/OPO mode, done in May 1980 – loads up at Muswell Hill Broadway on route 244's rush hour extension to Golders Green in the evening of 15 October 1981. Until RT to SMS OPO conversion in January 1971, the route had been extended to Highgate and Archway Station in rush hours instead. Now in its last few months of operation, it saw a mixture of D/DMSs, LSs and Metrobuses working it until withdrawal in the spring of 1982. This vehicle had entered service at Cricklewood in April 1978, moved to South East London in February 1982, then took four months to overhaul between July and November that year. It ended up, as most B20s did, in South West London, initially at Sutton, until withdrawal in July 1991. It saw three years' further use in Scotland before going for scrap.

*Above*: **Also in** my home area, on 23 October 1981, Walthamstow DMS1841 arrives at Turnpike Lane Station with destination blind set for the return to Ilford already. It had been new to the garage in June 1975, replacing MBs on routes 275 and 276, and still looks smart after May 1981 overhaul. As the new Titan following shows, DMSs at the garage were progressively being replaced by that type – this one moved to Thornton Heath in February 1982, ending up for a couple of months at the new Plumstead Garage before Titans ousted it there too in January 1984, after which it never ran again. At the time of this picture, the 144 was worked by three different types of OPO double-decker, since DMSs at its other garage, Wood Green, were being gradually replaced there too, but by new Metrobuses.

*Opposite above*: **On the** same occasion, DMS422 lumbers its way past Turnpike Lane Station into Wood Green High Road on training duties. It had entered service replacing SMSs at Ponders End Garage on route 107 in September 1972, and been demoted in January 1978. After disposal by LT, it survived a little longer as a staff bus for Durham coal miners operated by Bedlington & District. Many DMSs were used to replace some of the last RTs on training duties in 1978/79, as well as a number of RMs and RMLs which were returned to service, some of them effectively replacing DMSs as in the case of route 106.

*Opposite below*: **The influx** of new Metrobuses at Wood Green Garage also ended the use of DMSs on trolleybus replacement route 221. On 29 October 1981, their DMS2075 heads south at Manor House Station. It wrongly shows a via blind for the Turnpike Lane to Edgware section of the route, which still operates at the time of writing. This one had been new in May 1975 at Romford North Street Garage, from where it was ousted by new Titans in February 1980 and sent to Wood Green. A couple of days after I took this picture, it moved east again to Poplar, but was withdrawn in January 1982, again replaced by Titans. It was later exported to Hong Kong.

From A to B..
PRIVATE
..to C to D to..
CAMB

WATNEYS
How can you save money on bus fares?
221
HOLBORN CIRCUS
Pass
KJD 75P

*Above*: **Just arrived** at Stamford Hill for route 67 from Wood Green, DMS1615 approaches its Leman Street terminus beneath the murky arches of the London, Tilbury & Southend line in Aldgate on 30 October 1981. This one had been new to Edmonton, initially working as a crew bus on route 149, in February 1974. After shifting to various garages following arrival of purpose-built DMs there, it was overhauled to Wood Green in March 1981. Ousted by new Metrobuses for a second time, it was resettled from Stamford Hill to South West London in June 1982, working at such garages as Merton and South Croydon until withdrawn in July 1983, never to run again.

*Opposite above*: **Not far** away, also on 30 October 1981, Camberwell DMS2083 is on the opening part of Tower Bridge as it heads for home on the short route 42. The mind boggles to ponder what might have happened if the bridge had opened as one of these contraptions was crossing (or the MBs and SMSs which previously worked the route), and the vehicle had had to jump the gap. Unlike an RT which survived such a mishap in 1952, their flimsy bodywork would probably have been wrecked, with disastrous results for the driver and passengers. Briefly used at Poplar when new in June 1976, this DMS otherwise spent its entire, short LT life at Camberwell, being withdrawn when ousted by new Titans in August 1982, and was another of many DMs and DMSs exported for further service in Hong Kong afterwards.

*Opposite below*: **Having entered** service in May 1976, the unfortunate DMS1977 was displaced by new Metrobuses at Uxbridge, Fulwell and Hendon garages before being sent to Wood Green in February 1980. On a sunny Guy Fawkes Day, 1981, it changes driver opposite the garage when working route 298. Overhauled in April 1982, it moved south to Catford Garage, surviving the changes of the following September to move on to New Cross. Following withdrawal in January 1984, it saw further London service with Metrobus of Orpington on LRT contracts, finally being exported to the USA and used as a sightseeing bus in New York.

42
CAMBERWELL GREEN
KJD 83 P

The greatest name in King Size
298
TURNPIKE LANE STN
DMS 1977
KUC 977P

*Above*: **At the** same period, gradual replacement of DMSs was also well in hand on the other side of the River Lea. Titans were gradually replacing the large allocation of them at Walthamstow Garage, and on a soggy 21 November 1981, DMS1858 loads up at the town's Central bus station. After entering service briefly at Bromley in June 1975, it spent its entire (and again short) LT life here, having initially been used to replace MBs on routes 275 and 276. Withdrawn a week or two after I photographed it on the former route, it never ran again.

*Opposite above*: **Also loading** at Walthamstow Central Bus Station that day, DMS813 had entered service at Edmonton in February 1974, later seeing use at various South London garages before having a long-drawn-out Aldenham overhaul, from which it emerged to Walthamstow Garage in April 1981, explaining why it still looks quite smart in this picture. It too was expelled from there by Titans a week or two later, but returned to South London where it lasted until July 1983. It also ended up as a sightseeing bus in the USA.

*Opposite below*: **On the** same day, the weather is equally dreary at Chingford Mount, Prince Albert, where DMS2119, also from Walthamstow, loads up on route 276. This one had entered service at Catford in July 1976, moving to Edgware in July 1980 and then, upon replacement by Metrobuses, to what would prove to be its last LT garage only four months later. The vehicle was withdrawn in January 1982, after just five and a half years' LT service. However, it saw further use with various British operators before being exported to the USA in 1993 for use as a New York sightseeing bus.

34
BARNET
DMS 813
TGX 813M

OLIVIA
NEWTON-JOHN
NEW ALBUM
PHYSICAL
Chingford Road
Chingford Mount
Mansfield Hill
276
CHINGFORD
FHW
BUS STOP
276
97
PLEASE PAY AS YOU ENTER
KJD119P

***Above:*** **Also at** Chingford Mount that day, DMS2202 waits to turn right from Chingford Road into New Road on route 97A, a new service introduced to partially replace route W21 the previous January. Entering service at Merton and then South Croydon in February 1977, this one had been transferred to Walthamstow to replace RTs on route 34 in September that year. Yet another ousted from there by new Titans in December 1981, it saw further use at Putney Garage before Metrobuses replaced it there, and its withdrawal in May 1983. It had a much longer life with various non-London operators after that, lasting until 2000.

***Opposite above:*** **Advert-less DMS1625** gleams in the rain on the stand at Chingford Mount as its intending passengers wait in it until its driver is ready to open the doors and load up on route 158, another new route introduced at the end of January 1981. It replaced the northern end of route 58. New in March 1974, this DMS saw brief use at Bow before moving to Ponders End Garage, later working from Edmonton and South Croydon before overhaul to Walthamstow in April 1981. Replaced there by new Titans in January 1982, it returned to Croydon until replacement by newer B20 DMSs in April 1983. It never ran again after that. The Routemasters behind it had (numerically) begun working in this area back in early 1960, and still had a good few years ahead of it – what a contrast.

*Right*: **Yet another** new route introduced in the Walthamstow and Chingford areas at the end of January 1981, route 97 replaced the northern section of route 69, running between Leyton, Downsell Road and Chingford Station, where DMS1877 has terminated also on 21 November 1981. Interestingly, much of its route had originally been tram route 97, which trolleybus route 697 replaced in the late 1930s. This DMS entered service at Bromley Garage in July 1975, moving to Romford North Street the following month. It was overhauled to Walthamstow in May 1981 and displaced there by new Titans in January 1982. Sent south to Thornton Heath, it was withdrawn in October 1983 and saw various non-PSV use after disposal.

*Above*: **Another new** route introduced amid Walthamstow's January 1981 changes was the 212, replacing parts of the W21 circular service. Also at Chingford Station, DMS1855 is set to run back to its garage. Briefly used at Wood Green, this was another new for replacement of Walthamstow's MBs on routes 275 and 276 in June 1975, and was one of the last DMSs to leave the garage when finally ousted by Titans in March 1982. It moved to New Cross, being withdrawn from there in January 1984. It saw further use with various other operators until as late as 1996.

*Opposite above*: **The days** of early DMSs such as DMS8 were very much numbered at London's service by this time, and also at Chingford Station on 21 November 1981, it only lasted at Potters Bar Garage for a couple of weeks longer before withdrawal. It had entered service at the beginning of January 1971 on route 220 at Shepherd's Bush Garage, remaining there until Aldenham overhaul, from which it emerged after several months in June 1978. It had been at Potters Bar since October 1980 and, somewhat sadly, finally went for scrap in 1984 after more than two years, unwanted, in store.

*Opposite below*: **As related** earlier, in 1977/78, Ponders End Garage's earlier DMSs were replaced by new B20 examples, which also replaced RTs directly there on routes 217 and 217B in August 1977. On 22 November 1981, DMS2506 has terminated on route 107 at Edgware Station, where it is accompanied by that garage's Metrobuses. It had been new to Cricklewood Garage in January 1978, moving north in July 1980 following replacement by Ms, which would also oust them from Ponders End Garage not long after I took this picture. Taken from there to Aldenham for overhaul in February 1982, it took until July that year to deal with, whereupon it was banished to Brixton Garage. It lasted in South West London until April 1992, latterly as a trainer, and saw brief use with Maybury Coaches after sale.

GOODBYE PORK PIE
Waltham Abbey
Waltham + Cheshunt
Cuffley Potters Bar
242
WALTHAM CROSS
GOODBYE PORK PIE
FARES FAIR
EGP 8J
Station

Edgware Elstree
Borehamwood
Barnet Enfield
107
ENFIELD LOCK
New
Extra Long
Marlboro 100's
to a Guinness
THX506S

*Above*: **Heavy snowfall** struck North London overnight on the night of 10/11 December 1981, with this result for the morning rush hour. DMS2515, another Ponders End B20, battles through the blizzard at Edmonton, Cambridge roundabout on route 231. It was literally quicker for me to walk from there to Turnpike Lane (where the DMS is going) than use the bus on my way to 'work'. This DMS' history mirrors that of 2506 above, until May 1982 overhaul when it was outshopped to Bexleyheath. It lasted until July 1991, and then spent some five years in service with Maynes of Manchester.

*Opposite above*: **In Westbury** Avenue, Wood Green, about half an hour later, traffic is jammed solid in both directions as DMS2494 on the same route attempts to get home to Ponders End Garage. This B20 had been new there in December 1977, leaving for overhaul in January 1982. It was outshopped to Wandsworth the following April, lasting until October 1992. After that, it was exported to Hong Kong.

*Opposite below*: **Also stuck** in Westbury Avenue on sister route 217 that snowbound morning, DMS2330 is the one illustrated earlier on route 34, which had spent much of its early life in store. It left Ponders End for overhaul in March 1982, emerging to Merton Garage three months later. It was an early withdrawal for the type, in July 1990, and never ran again.

231
PONDERS END GARAGE
231
THX 494S

POLICE
217
TURNPIKE LANE STN
KEYS CUT
THX 330S

*Above:* **Next day,** 12 December 1981, snow is still very much in evidence at Lower Edmonton Station, where Edmonton DMS715 is one of two heading south on route 259 and has been curtailed at Finsbury Park, perhaps owing to the bad weather. It had been new to Alperton Garage in October 1973, replacing MBs, and seven years later upon CoF expiry received a three-year recertification, whereupon it moved to Edmonton. Ousted from there by Metrobuses in June 1982, it was sent south to Thornton Heath where it expired in October 1983, thus just about achieving ten years at London's service before withdrawal and scrapping. A better London innings than many of its class.

*Opposite above*: **On the** same day, Edmonton DMS1969 is at the junction of Church Street and Haslebury Road in Upper Edmonton, working route W8. Used initially for a day or two at Upton Park when new in May 1976, it then replaced SMSs on route 112 at Stonebridge Park, going to Aldenham for overhaul when that garage closed in August 1981. It is still smartly turned out after being outshopped to Edmonton in October. Metrobuses also replaced it there in June 1982, when it was sent to South Croydon. It was withdrawn in November 1983, and was another which never ran again.

*Opposite below*: **Further snowfall** struck North London on 21 December 1981, when Walthamstow DMS2176 heads for home from Turnpike Lane Bus Station in the morning rush hour on route 144. Briefly used at Poplar when new in April 1976, it always otherwise ran from Walthamstow until ousted by new Titans six years later, and also never saw further use after withdrawal at that time.

FARES FAIR
10p 20p
30p 40p
W8
CHASE FARM HOSPITAL
FARES FAIR
KUC 969P

Building Soc
uilding Society
FARES FAIR
10p 20p
30p 40p
144
WALTHAMSTOW GARAGE
FARES FAIR
PLEASE PAY AS YOU ENTER
OJD 176R
INTER CITY CAM

*Above*: **On 30** December 1981, DMS1927, which had been overhauled to Holloway Garage the previous month, appears to be abandoned at the foot of Highgate Hill when working route 271. This is perhaps due to a staff cut, and there was an inspector nearby to keep his eye on it. The vehicle had been new to Upton Park in November 1975, and was withdrawn from Holloway in September 1983, seeing very brief further use with Midland Red before going for scrap. My once local route 271 suffered the ignominy of being one of the routes to be DMS-operated the longest in North London, from January 1971 until the spring of 1984. This long-standing trolleybus replacement route was withdrawn in February 2023.

*Opposite above*: **Just around** the corner that day in Archway Road, DMS1934 is another that had been overhauled to Holloway Garage, in October 1981. It works their weekend allocation on route 263, extended on Saturdays and Sundays from Archway Station to King's Cross replacing route 17. It had been new in November 1975 to Finchley Garage (where it also worked the 263), moving to Clapton five years later upon ousting by Metrobuses. It too was withdrawn in September 1983, but survived to see further use with various operators until as late as 1999.

*Opposite below*: **North London** has had another dusting of snow as Holloway DMS154 heads south along Ilsedon Road from Finsbury Park on 11 January 1982. Route 168A no longer usually served this road by then, having been diverted away from it to terminate at Hornsey Rise. However, an obstruction in Hornsey Road meant southbound buses had to be diverted via the old routeing. This DMS had entered service at Fulwell replacing RMs on route 267 in September 1971, and was overhauled to Holloway in October 1978. It was withdrawn in July 1982 and was yet another never to run again.

263
KINGS CROSS
KUC 934P
FARE FAIR

168A
WATERLOO
JGF 154K
UTM 99W

*Above*: **An oddity** to appear on route 35 on 23 January 1982, subbing for RMs, is Camberwell DM1113, by now usually used there as a spare for them on route 172. It arrives at Clapton Pond, to where the route had recently been extended from Hackney Station. DMs and DMSs were never scheduled to work it, the route being converted to Titan OPO in June 1986. The DM had been new to Camberwell for the 172's conversion from RT at the end of August 1975, and remained there until withdrawal in June 1982. It subsequently saw use as a London sightseeing bus with independent operators before being exported to the USA in 1987.

*Opposite above*: **On 2** February 1982, Ponders End B20 DMS2412 crosses the junction of Southbury Road and the Great Cambridge Road working local route 135, which had been the last at its garage using RTs when converted to RM operation in January 1978; DMS OPO followed in September 1980. New to Ponders End in the summer of 1977, it went to Aldenham for overhaul a week or two after I took this picture, not emerging until August when it was sent to Catford. Withdrawn in January 1992, it also saw further use as a London sightseeing bus until 2005, subsequently spending a couple of years in the same role in Glasgow.

*Opposite below*: **Outside Ponders** End Garage itself on the same occasion are DMS2406, which we have already encountered, and DMS2487. Of note is the differing position of their registration plates. The latter was new to the garage in December 1977, and upon displacement by new Metrobuses, one of which is visible on the left, migrated to Sutton Garage in March 1982. It was withdrawn ten years later, seeing a few months' service with Midland Fox thereafter until January 1994. Route 217B, for which it is blinded, was later renumbered 317.

135
CARTERHATCH
OJD412R

Waltham Abbey
Waltham Cross
Great Cambridge Road
217B
PONDERS END GARAGE
From A to B...
135
PONDERS END GARAGE
From A to B...
THX 487S
OJD406R

*Above:* **Back at** the nearby junction of Southbury Road with the A10, Edmonton DMS1449 crosses on route 191, on which the type had replaced RTs in the spring of 1974. Of note is the 'No Entry' cordon across where these vehicles' automatic fare collection equipment was. By now, because so few people used these contraptions, which often broke down anyway, they were taken out of use on DMSs, thereby forcing passengers to pay their drivers, exacerbating their already excruciatingly slow boarding times. They also wasted space, and some vehicles later had seats placed where they had been, as on crew-operated DMs. This DMS had been new to Upton Park Garage for route 173 in June 1973, receiving an overhaul to Willesden Garage in November 1978. It was displaced by Metrobuses there in June 1980 and sent to Edmonton. When the same fate befell it there two years later, it was withdrawn, ending up owned for at least ten years by the Harlow Majorettes.

*Opposite above:* **Over in** South West London, the area where the last DMSs were to work at London's service ten or eleven years later, Merton DMS2016 sets off from Clapham Common, terminus of route 131's Sunday extension replacing weekday route 155, for West Moseley on 14 February 1982. The 131 had received DMSs in May 1973, but this one was new in September 1976 to Seven Kings Garage, being displaced by Titans and sent south west in May 1980. It perished in the September 1982 'Law Lords' rulings but saw further service with various operators until 1990.

*Opposite below:* **Back in** my home area, Wood Green DM1246 loads up just south of Manor House Station on route 141 on 23 February 1982, at a time when the route was being gradually re-converted to RM operation. Initially used on the RLST, it moved to Chalk Farm for the 24 in October 1976, being swapped with Stonebridge Park's RMLs on the 18 in April 1979. Ousted by new Metrobuses there in June 1980, it was then sent to Wood Green where it also perished in September 1982. After that, it survived to see some ten years' further use with Midland Red East and its successor, Midland Fox.

Hampton Court
Kingston Wimbledon
Tooting Balham
131
WEST MOLESEY
From
A to B...
...to C
to D to...
BOOKERS
FOR
BARGAINS
BOOKERS FOR BARGAINS
PLEASE PAY AS YOU ENTER
KJD 16 P

Best taste.
Best buy!
NESCAFE
Turnpike Lane Stn
Green Lanes
City Road
141
MOORGATE
DM1246
KUC 246P

*Above*: **Moving comfortably** ahead from their replacement of Walthamstow Garage's DMSs, some of the next victims of new Titans in the East were at West Ham Garage. On 27 February 1982, their DMS1628 approaches its terminus at Stratford Broadway on trolleybus replacement route 278, which had once continued north to Walthamstow and Chingford. New to Barking in February 1974, it had been overhauled to West Ham in June 1981, and moved to Walworth following replacement by Titans in July 1982. Sent on to Battersea two months later, it was withdrawn in June 1983, later being exported to the USA.

*Opposite above*: **An early** DMS still active from West Ham Garage that day is DMS139, heading along The Grove, Stratford on route 241, a new route introduced with RMs on 7 September 1968 (replacing parts of the 123 and 41) and converted to DMS in June 1973. It was new to Brixton Garage for route 50 in July 1971, and overhauled to West Ham in November 1978. It was withdrawn a few days after I took this picture, and never ran again.

*Opposite below*: **On the** same occasion, Bow DMS378 is also in Stratford, running around the one-way system bound for Wanstead on route 10, a once important trunk route whose decline was accelerated by conversion from RT to DMS at the end of October 1972. This one had been new at Wandsworth to convert route 44 from RT in June of that year, moving to Bow upon overhaul in September 1978. Replaced there by new Titans in August 1982, it too never ran again.

Plaistow Broadway
Balaam Street
Freemasons Road
241
CANNING TOWN
WORLD LEADER
Rothmans King Size
the best tobacco
money can buy
W. WAIDE POLLARD & SONS
PLEASE PAY AS YOU ENTER
JGF 139K

Aldgate Bow
Stratford Wanstead
10
WANSTEAD STATION
PLEASE PAY AS YOU ENTER
JGF 378K

*Above*: **Graphically illustrating** the gradual change from DMS to Titan operation in the East at this period, West Ham DMS2128 on route 262 is followed by a brand-new Titan at Leyton, Bakers Arms junction also on 27 February 1982. It had been new to Ponders End Garage in October 1976, then displaced to West Ham by new B20s there the following June. It was withdrawn a few days after I took this picture, but lasted with various new operators until 1997.

*Opposite above*: **With a** pair of recently introduced Titans for company on the same day, West Ham DMS36 sets off for the Docks on route 262 from Walthamstow Central Bus Station. New to Shepherd's Bush Garage for route 220 in January 1971, it was overhauled to West Ham in June 1978 and withdrawn there in April 1982. However, this early DMS survived in use with various subsequent operators well into the 1990s.

*Opposite below*: **Although Clapham** Garage had been reopened operationally in April 1981 while Norwood Garage was being rebuilt, it still had plenty of space to store withdrawn DMSs. On 28 February 1982, DMS2014 is amongst a group of them, having been new to Loughton Garage for route 20A in September 1976, and displaced by new Titans there to Merton Garage for a few days in February 1982 prior to withdrawal. It did, however, see about ten years' further use with subsequent operators.

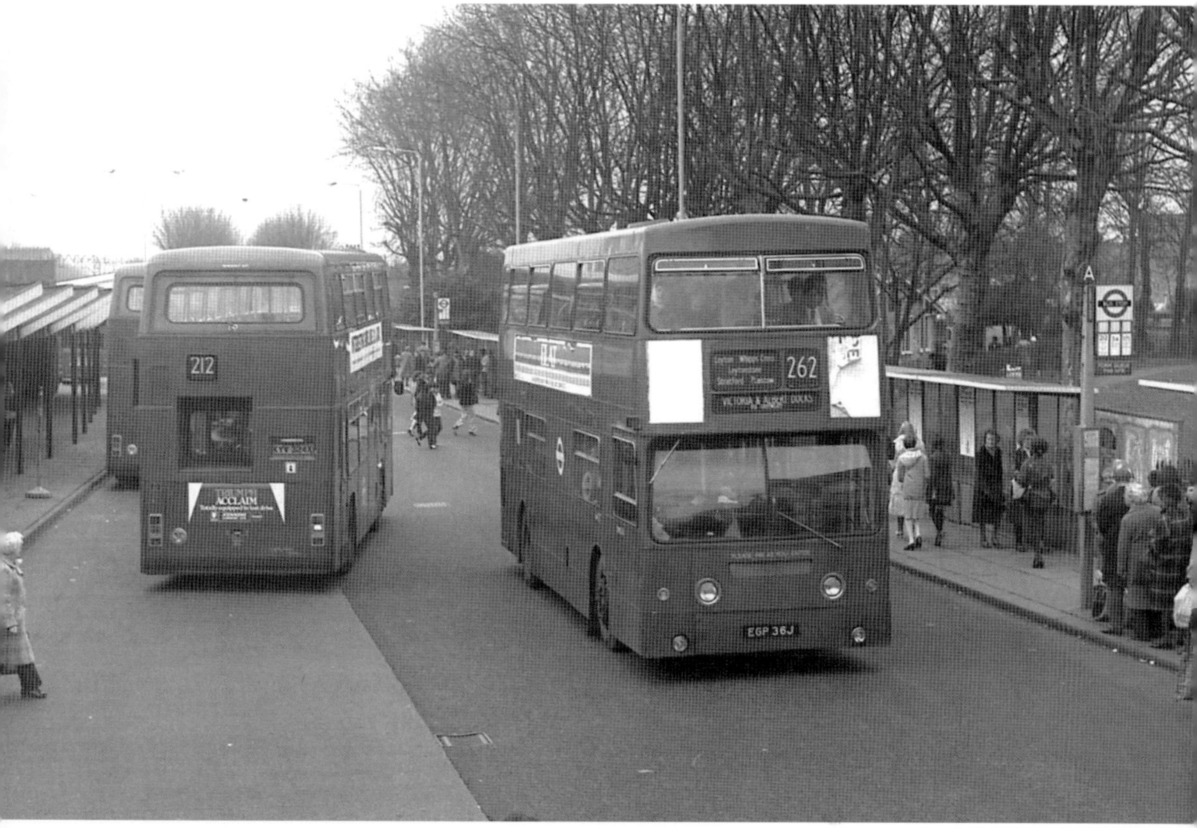
212
262
ACCLAIM
EGP 36J

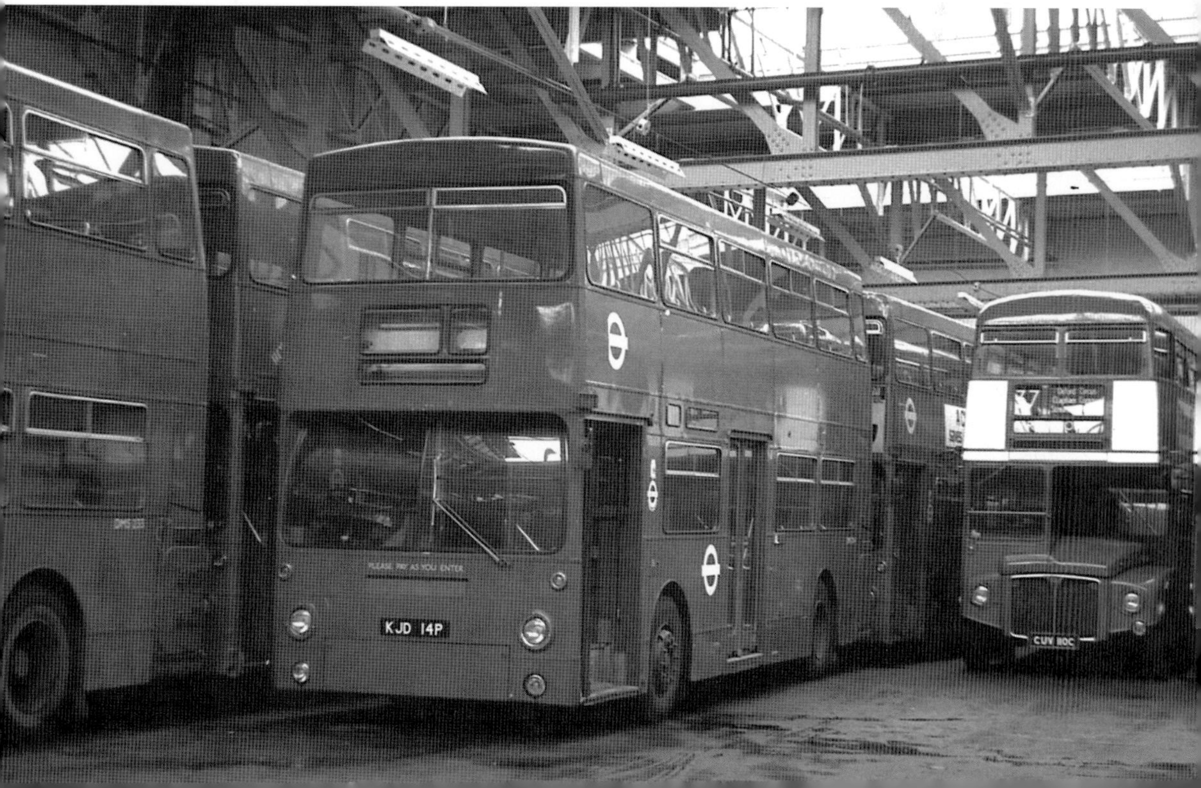
KJD 14P

*Above:* **A strange** contraption tucked away in the depths of Clapham Garage that day is the remains of DMS2172, a fire victim in September 1980 at Catford Garage, cut down to become an instruction chassis for the benefit of apprentice fitters. It had been new to Elmers End Garage in December 1976, moving to Catford two months later. It was eventually sold to Paddington Technical College in June 1983. Another oddity on the right is long-dead MBS217, also retained for instruction purposes.

*Opposite above:* **By this** period, the early DMSs on one of their two pioneer routes, the 220, had been replaced by later examples at Shepherd's Bush Garage. As dusk falls, also on 28 February 1982, their DMS1953 collects passengers at the southern end of Putney Bridge bound for Tooting. It was new to Hanwell Garage in December 1975, replacing MBSs, moving to Catford when displaced by Metrobuses in June 1981. Overhauled four months later to Potters Bar, it was again displaced by them the following December and transferred to Shepherd's Bush. The upheavals of September 1982 saw it moved to Putney Garage. In May 1983, it moved north again to Holloway and was then demoted to training duties six months later. After a few years in such use, and then a long period in store, it was cannibalised for spare parts early in 1990.

*Opposite below:* **DMS68 had** entered service at Merton on route 189 at the end of January 1971. Overhauled (after the customary several months in Aldenham) in August 1978, it was transferred to Holloway Garage a year later, and is still there on 5 March 1982 when terminating at Archway Station on route 239. Six months later, it was one of the many standard DMSs that perished as a result of the cuts, and yet another that never ran again.

TDK
THE GREAT NAME IN TAPE CASSETTES.
DARYL HALL
220
TOOTING STN
JOHN OATES
DMS 1953
KUC 953P

DARYL HALL
PRIVATE EYES
Dartmouth Park Hill
York Way Kings Cross
Euston Kingsway
239
ARCHWAY STATION
JOHN OATES
AQUARIUS
EMPLOYMENT BUREAU
PLEASE PAY AS YOU ENTER
EGP 68J

*Above*: **By this** time, DMSs at Loughton Garage are also falling by the wayside owing to replacement by new Titans. But on 6 March 1982, DMS2177 is one of two heading south along Loughton High Road. The class had replaced SMSs on route 167, which in turn ousted RTs in July 1971. New in December 1976, this one worked briefly at Leyton Garage and then moved to Walthamstow, where it remained until replaced by Titans in January 1982 when it moved to Loughton. Its stay there was brief, however, since shortly after I took this picture, it was also replaced there by Titans. Unusually, it then became an Aldenham Works staff bus, usually outstationed at London Country's Tring Garage for the run to Aylesbury. It remained in such use until Aldenham's closure in the autumn of 1986, then 'after a brief spell serving Chiswick Works' sold. It survived in various non-PSV roles until 2005.

*Opposite above*: **The one** behind in the previous picture is their DMS1618, which still looks smart when on route 20A. DMSs replaced RTs directly on this route in October 1976. It had entered service at Barking Garage in February 1974, being ousted from there too by Titans in June 1980 and sent to Thornton Heath. It was overhauled to Loughton in April 1981, and history repeated itself a week or two after I took this picture, when Titans displaced it to Thornton Heath again. It lasted there until September 1983, when it was withdrawn. It never ran again.

*Opposite below*: **Looking very** shabby indeed, Stamford Hill DMS146 calls at route 67's first stop southbound at Spouter's Corner, Wood Green on 24 March 1982. The 67 had converted from RM to DMS in December 1971, but this one had entered service three months previously at Fulwell on route 267. It was overhauled to Stamford Hill in November 1978, and yet another withdrawn from 4 September 1982, also one that never ran again too.

BUSINESS TRAVEL
PLEASURE TRAVEL
Epping Forest Loughton
Woodford Wells
Sth Woodford Wanstead
20A
LEYTONSTONE GREEN MAN
STH.WOODFORD. 989 9445
ABBOTTS TRAVEL
LOUGHTON. 508 2295
PLEASE PAY AS YOU ENTER
KML 499P
THM 618M

St. Ann's Hospital
Stamford Hill
Dalston Shoreditch
67
ALDGATE
The greatest name in King Size
PLEASE PAY AS YOU ENTER
JGF 146K

*Above*: **Next day,** 25 March 1982, a visit to Aldenham Works finds B20 DMS2481 and DMS2484 awaiting intake to overhaul. Both had entered service when new at Palmers Green Garage replacing RTs on route 34 in September 1977, being transferred to Ponders End upon replacement by Metrobuses in October 1981. It is of note that their overhaul intake, in common with most B20s, is ahead of not only their fifth 'birthdays' in service, but two years ahead of the usual seven years for new vehicles. Was this because LT didn't trust them to last a full seven year CoF spell without overhaul? As it was, they took until June and July 1992 respectively to overhaul, both being sent to Catford Garage. DMS2481 was withdrawn in November 1991, and saw a further four years' use with various operators. DMS2484 did slightly better, lasting until March 1992 with LT and then as late as the mid-2000s with other owners.

*Opposite above*: **A very** odd working on 9 April 1982 is West Ham DMS2230 on usually RM-operated 58, when arriving at its Walthamstow, Crooked Billet terminus. By the time this route converted to OPO in the autumn of that year, Titans had replaced West Ham's DMSs. This one, apart from a few days beforehand at Merton and Poplar, had entered service there in June 1977, yet was withdrawn in September 1982. It survived with various other operators until 1991.

*Opposite below*: **Also on** 9 April 1982, Bow DMS48 has arrived at Victoria Station on route 10. New to Brixton Garage for the second 'pioneer' DMS route, the 95, at the beginning of January 1971, it was overhauled to Bow Garage in July 1978. Displaced there by new Titans in September 1982, it survived another three months in service at Battersea before withdrawal. At London Transport's Golden Jubilee weekend public open days at Chiswick Works in July 1983, it was wrecked as a result of being used for 'turnover bus' demonstrations.

YOU'LL FIND IT FASTER-BECAUSE IT'S MORE LOCAL
58
WALTHAMSTOW
OJD 230R
PMU 744R

Elephant London Bdg
Aldgate Bow
Stratford Wanstead
10
WANSTEAD STATION
From A to B...
...to C to D to...
DECREASE THE INCREASE GET A BUS PASS
BUS PASS
PLEASE PAY AS YOU ENTER
EGP 48J
KEEP LEFT
L.T.E.

*Above*: **Oddly displaying** two offside LT roundels, Holloway DMS837 passes beneath the North London Line in Camden Gardens on 15 April 1982, and is unusually curtailed at King's Cross on trolleybus replacement route 214. This was one of several of Holloway's routes converted to crew DM operation in 1975, and whereas most of the others went over to RM operation between 1977 and 1982, this one changed to DMS OPO in 1981. The DMS was new to the RLST at Stockwell in May 1974, moving to Holloway five months later. It remained there until perishing amid the September 1982 Law Lords' service cuts, never to run again.

*Opposite above*: **Sutton Garage** was to become one of the last bastions of DMS operation in the early 1990s, using B20 examples, but in the spring of 1982 still had earlier ones. On 18 April, their DMS271 is at route 293's Epsom High Street terminus. It had been new to replace RTs on route 177 at New Cross Garage in January 1972, being overhauled to Sutton in April 1979. It was withdrawn in June 1982 and was yet another never to run again afterwards.

*Opposite below*: **A newer** DMS working from Sutton that day is DMS2052, heading south through Belmont, bound for Lower Kingswood. Its cramped destination blind looks decidedly odd, and it appears to be running empty. New in December 1976 to Alperton Garage, it moved in the same month to Uxbridge, from where it was displaced to Sutton by new Metrobuses in July 1981. Another withdrawn in September 1982, it then saw use with various other operators for a few years.

293
MORDEN STN
Katy Bell
JGF 271K

Sutton Common Rd
Sutton Belmont
Banstead
80
LOWER KINGSWOOD
PLEASE PAY AS YOU ENTER
OUC 52R

*Above*: **Also heading** south through Belmont that day, Sutton DMS1685 is bound for Epsom on route 164. It had been new to Holloway Garage in August 1974, moving to Bexleyheath and then Plumstead three months later. Displaced by MDs in April 1980, it ended up at Sutton, from where it was withdrawn in July 1982. It is another that never ran again after withdrawal by LT, after less than eight years' service.

*Opposite above*: **Pursued by** an RM on route 104, Muswell Hill B20 crew DM2629 heads south along Holloway Road from the famous Nag's Head junction on 21 April 1982. New to Cricklewood Garage in June 1978, it was transferred to Muswell Hill in August 1980, in both cases replacing earlier DMs. Amongst the many results of the service cuts of 4 September 1982, route 43 reverted to RM operation (having previously converted from RML to crew DM in January 1975) but the 104 converted from RM to DMS OPO. The two routes ran together all the way from Highgate Station to Moorgate, and OPO conversion was the death knell for the once-important route 104, which was withdrawn just under three years later. The DM was sent south to Croydon upon the change, where it was adopted as a 'show bus' commemorating LT's Golden Jubilee in 1983.

*Opposite below*: **Route 134,** which also paralleled the 43 between Friern Barnet and Archway Station, had been one of the first to receive crew DMs, having suffered them since the autumn of 1973. It too reverted to RM on 4 September 1982. Also on 21 April that year, Potters Bar DM1714 passes through Muswell Hill. Used briefly at Cricklewood when new in October 1974, the rest of its short life was spent on this route at Potters Bar Garage until its withdrawal in July 1982. It too never ran again.

The greatest name in King Size
43
LONDON BRIDGE STN
104
MOORGATE
THX 629S

CHECKMATE
134
TOTTENHAM CT RD STN
THM 714M

*Above:* **Next day,** 22 April 1982, a cluster of DMSs outside Sutton Station typifies the fleet based at that town's LT garage. Nearest the camera, DMS249 heads for Epsom on route 164. Withdrawn a few days later, it had been new to Walworth Garage in December 1971, moving to Abbey Wood the following month to convert route 177 from RT operation. It went to Sutton upon overhaul in April 1979, never to run again after withdrawal. DMS191 on the right, which has terminated on route 80A, was new to Bexleyheath to replace RTs on route 96 in November 1971, was overhauled to Sutton in February 1979, and although yet another of the victims of the Law Lords' cuts, being withdrawn in September 1982, ...survived... in non-PSV use into the 2000s.

*Opposite above:* **On the** same day, Battersea DMS338 sets off from Putney Heath Green Man terminus on route 39, which had received the type to replace RTs in July 1972. It had been new to Peckham Garage replacing RTs on route 78 in May that year and was overhauled to Battersea in June 1979. It was withdrawn in July 1982 and also never ran again. Once an important trunk route linking Southfields with Tottenham and Edmonton, the 39 by now ventured no further north than Victoria but had received an extension beyond Southfields to Putney.

*Opposite below:* **A ride** to the East on 23 April 1982 finds Poplar DMS844 crossing the northern approaches to Blackwall Tunnel when running in to its garage on route 277, having traversed the route's Isle of Dogs loop. New to Merton Garage in May 1974, it quickly moved to Alperton, where it was displaced by new Metrobuses in July 1980. Sent to Wood Green as a result, they ousted it there too in October 1981 when it was sent to Poplar. It was withdrawn in July 1982 and was yet another destined only for the scrapyard afterwards. Trolleybus replacement route 277 had converted from RT to DMS in January 1974, these being gradually replaced by Titans in the summer of 1982.

Chelsea Battersea
Clapham Junction
Wandsworth
39
VICTORIA
JGF 338K

Essex Road Dalston
Hackney Victoria Park
Mile End Cubitt Town
277
POPLAR (IRON BRIDGE) VIA
PLEASE PAY AS YOU ENTER
TGX 844M

*Above*: **Traditional London** bus route 56 had served the Isle of Dogs loop for many years, at one time running from Mile End Station to Blackwall Tunnel and Poplar via Cubitt Town. From its introduction in April 1959, however, route 277 gradually supplanted it, until the 56 was withdrawn completely in October 1969. The route was revived for a few years in the 1980s but continued from Limehouse to Aldgate. Also on 23 April 1982, Poplar DMS815 has turned short at Limehouse, and sets off for the latter point. Used briefly as a crew bus on route 149 at Edmonton when new in February 1974, it then worked at various garages before overhaul to Poplar in April 1981. Displaced by new Titans there in June 1982, it was transferred to Merton Garage from where it was withdrawn in September 1983, after which it never saw further use.

*Opposite above*: **Also at** the junction of Commercial Road and Burdett Road in Limehouse, Poplar DMS1424 is about to embark on its trip around the Isle of Dogs. Its driver seems to be amused at having his bus photographed. This DMS had been new to Thornton Heath Garage in April 1973 and 'following a three-year recertification' was reallocated to Walworth in June 1980, moving to Poplar the following December. Withdrawn in July 1982, it saw use with various other operators until 1988. As for route 56, it had been reintroduced in June 1980, and lasted until November 1987 when it was rendered superfluous by the new Docklands Light Railway.

*Opposite below*: **On the** same day as the previous three pictures, Bow DMS332 has just set off from Wanstead Station, and passes George Green on its way to Victoria. New to Wandsworth Garage in June 1972 replacing RTs on route 44, it was overhauled to Bow for route 10 in August 1979. It is yet another that was withdrawn on 4 September 1982, never to run again.

Commercial Road
Limehouse
Cubitt Town Poplar
56
ISLE OF DOGS AND LIMEHOUSE
YOU'LL FIND IT FASTER-BECAUSE IT'S MORE LOCAL
PLEASE PAY AS YOU ENTER
MLH 424L
MEN
EASTERN CA

Elephant London Bdg
Aldgate Bow
Stratford Wanstead
10
VICTORIA
PLEASE PAY AS YOU ENTER
JGF 332K
JPU372V
SUPPLIES
NCE

*Above*: **On 24** May 1982, DMS392 is at Aldwych working route 239 from Holloway Garage. This route had been introduced in March 1971, using SMSs, replacing the northern end of route 196. DMSs replaced them in November 1975. This one entered service at Finchley on route 263, replacing RMs, in July 1972, being overhauled to Romford North Street in September 1979 but ousted from there by new Titans soon afterwards. It too was withdrawn in September 1982 (at the same time as route 239) but saw further use with an independent operator in Stevenage in the mid-1980s.

*Opposite above*: **Back in** the East, Bow DMS2159 has just crossed Bow Bridge over the River Lea and is probably running in to its garage, perhaps owing to a staff cut on route 10 on 29 May 1982. It had entered service at Wandsworth in November 1976, moving to Uxbridge the following month. Transferred to Southall in September 1977, it was replaced there by new Metrobuses two years later and sent to Bow. Withdrawn in August 1982 following the arrival of new Titans there, it saw further use as a London sightseeing bus until 1988 after sale by LT.

*Opposite below*: **On the** same day, Clapton DMS1508 has just passed beneath the closed Burdett Road Station on the London, Tilbury & Southend Line when heading for the Isle of Dogs and Poplar on route 277. It had entered service at Merton Garage in September 1973, moving to Clapton after a three-year recert in November 1980. Displaced by new Titans amid the September 1982 changes, it was transferred to Chalk Farm Garage, but withdrawn in February 1983. It never ran again.

10
BOW CHURCH
OJD 159 R

15-0
GENESIS
OUT NOW
277
POPLAR
DOUBLE LIVE
TDK
THE GREAT NAME IN TAPE CASSETTES
THM 508M

*Above*: **Outside Clapton** Garage itself later that day, their DMS1910 has just changed drivers on route 22A, a new service introduced with the type in October 1972. It had entered service at Romford North Street in September 1975, moving to Potters Bar the same month. Transferred to Catford and then Thornton Heath in November 1979, it was overhauled to Clapton in September 1981. Ousted by new Titans there in August 1982, it returned south to Merton, and finally South Croydon, only to be withdrawn less than two years after its overhaul, in July 1983, being yet another never to see service again.

*Opposite*: **On Sunday** 30 May 1982, my two little daughters Felicity (in pushchair) and Margaret have had a bumpy ride on Muswell Hill crew DM2599 from our home area to Chingford Station, for a ramble through nearby Epping Forest. By now, this garage only worked route 102 on Sundays, with Palmers Green RMs being its main daily allocation. The route converted to Metrobus OPO on 4 September, whereupon Muswell Hill's small share of it ceased, and it was thus never worked by OPO DMSs. This DM had been new to Cricklewood Garage in July 1978, moving to Muswell Hill in May 1980. The reversion of route 43 and 134 to RM operation (on the same day as the 102's OPO conversion) saw it transferred to Merton Garage, and it survived until December 1991.

Muswell Hill
Palmers Grn  Edmonton
Chingford Mount

102

CHINGFORD STATION

THX 599 S

*Above*: **By the** summer of 1982, replacement of DMSs by Metrobuses and Titans in West/North West/North London and East London respectively had progressed sufficiently that those in South East London were threatened with replacement by Titans too. On 1 June, Sidcup DMS2154 is at Green Street Green Common. New to the RLST in October 1976, it moved to Hornchurch, then Romford North Street in September 1977, being replaced there by Titans in May 1980 and sent to Barking where the same fate befell it two months later and it was exiled to Sidcup. Despite being less than six years old, it was withdrawn as a result of the September 1982 route cuts and exported to Hong Kong a month later. Route 51 had converted from RM to DMS operation in May 1977.

*Opposite above*: **It was** now just a matter of time before all early DMSs were withdrawn from LT service. Also on 1 June 1982, Catford DMS26 has just circumnavigated Camberwell Green on route 185's circuitous journey from Victoria to Forest Hill. This route had converted from RT to DMS in May 1973, this vehicle itself having been new to Shepherd's Bush for route 220's conversion from RM at the beginning of January 1971. Overhauled to West Ham in April 1978, it moved to Walthamstow after being displaced by Titans, and finally to Catford for the same reason. It was withdrawn later in June 1982, but survived with various other operators well into the 1990s.

*Opposite below*: **Also at** Camberwell Green that day, Walworth DMS117 is on fellow tram-replacement route 184, which had converted from RT to DMS in October 1971. This one was the final vehicle in their first batch, entering service at Brixton on route 50 in July that year. Overhauled in September 1978, it perished amid the September 1982 cuts and never ran again. Of note is its badly dented offside front lower corner, a common ailment of all the early LT OPO types produced in the late 1960s and 1970s.

185
FOREST HILL
CITY OFFICE·SALES
ANDREWS & ROBERTSON
LLOYDS CASHPOINT
PLEASE PAY AS YOU ENTER
EGP 26J

Elephant Camberwell
East Dulwich
Peckham Rye
184
ELEPHANT & CASTLE
PLEASE PAY AS YOU ENTER
EGP 117J

**Of the** same batch, DMS111 entered service at West Ham on route 5 in April 1971, and was overhauled in July 1978 to New Cross Garage, from which it works route 177 (another tram replacement service) in St. George's Road, Lambeth also on 1 June 1982. This one was withdrawn in August that year and also never ran again.

**An odd** working caught by my camera in Tulse Hill on 2 June 1982 is Stockwell B20 DM2587 subbing for an RM on route 2B. It had been new to Brixton Garage replacing earlier DMs in April 1978, displaced by the RM re-conversion of route 109 in August 1981 and usually used on the RLST. Latterly moved to Victoria Gillingham Street as part of the late 1980s LRT tours and charter fleet, it lasted until January 1992, being scrapped thereafter.

**Despite being** converted from crew DM to ex-Green Line RCL class coach Routemasters operation in the latter half of 1980, route 149 still received visits by DMs kept as RM/RCL spares until the summer of 1982. On 8 June, Edmonton DM1147 has been unusually curtailed at Stoke Newington Common. New to the 24 at Chalk Farm in October 1975, it switched to the 18 at Stonebridge Park in April 1979 in exchange for its RMLs. Transferred to Walworth in July 1980, it ended up at Edmonton in March 1981 and was withdrawn in July 1982. However, it saw further use with various operators as a London sightseeing bus, surviving until as late as 2008.

*Above*: **On the** same occasion, Stamford Hill DMS140 passes over Stoke Newington Common, having also been curtailed on route 67 to Shoreditch. It had been new for route 267 at Fulwell in September 1971, being overhauled to Stamford Hill in November 1978. It was withdrawn a few days after I took this picture, never to run again.

*Opposite above*: **At this** period, a number of B20 DMs allocated to Stockwell also put in odd appearances on normally RML-operated route 88. On 28 June 1982, RLST-branded DM2643, one of the last delivered, does so in Great Smith Street, Westminster in the evening rush hour. It too passed to LRT's tours and charter fleet, based at Victoria, and ended up converted to D crew/OPO configuration for its final five years of service. Withdrawn in March 1992, it saw further use with various fleets until 2001.

*Opposite below*: **The days** of Clapton DMS1441 at London's service are very much numbered on 13 July 1982, as it turns from Graham Road into Mare Street in Hackney town centre on route 277. It had entered service at Upton Park on route 173 in June 1973, receiving a three-year recert at nearby West Ham in April 1980, and being transferred to Clapton in August 1981. Among the hundreds of DMSs withdrawn as a result of the route cuts on 4 September 1982, it survived to see further use with various operators, initially in Scotland, until the late 1990s.

88
Shepherds Bush
Oxford St. Trafalgar Sq.
Clapham Tooting
88
CHARING CROSS
Round London Sightseeing Tour
THX643S

BRICKS
GENESIS
OUT NOW
POPLAR
277
GENESIS
DOUBLE LIVE
RUM
PLEASE PAY AS YOU ENTER
MLH 441L

*Above*: **Another DMS-operated** route which was actually withdrawn as a result of the route cuts was the 168A, on which Holloway DMS2058 approaches King's Cross Station on 28 July 1982, some six weeks beforehand. Its destination shows that it is running in service back to its garage, following route 41 from the 168A's usual Hornsey Rise terminus. This DMS entered service at Holloway in March 1976, surviving there until February 1984. It saw use with various other operators after sale.

*Opposite above*: **Four weeks** before its withdrawal due to the cuts, Putney DMS5 is at local route 264's Putney Bridge Station terminus on 7 August 1982, having recently moved there from Sutton Garage. It had served the same area when new to Shepherd's Bush for route 220 in January 1971, later having an Aldenham pilot overhaul that took from September 1977 to February 1978 to complete. It never ran again after withdrawal.

*Opposite below*: **Steep Dog** Kennel Hill in Dulwich was always a challenge for DMSs, especially when heavily loaded. On 20 August 1982, a fortnight before it perished in the cuts, Walworth DMS206 nears its summit on tram replacement route 184. It had entered service at Stamford Hill on route 67 in December 1971, moving away from there on overhaul in January 1979. After withdrawal, it too never ran again.

The fastest fusspots in the business.
Hoults Removals
Putney High Street
Upper Richmond Rd
Dover House Road
264
ROEHAMPTON
DMS 5
EGP 5J
PUTNEY
Fly to the plane.

184
BLACKFRIARS
JGF 206K

*Above*: **On the** same day, a very full Thornton Heath D1175 is on the one-way system at Brixton, St. Matthew's Church a fortnight before it too was withdrawn. The 109's Brixton share of route 109 had converted from crew DM back to RM in the summer of 1981, but Thornton Heath's share had to wait until September 1982. This DM had been new to Cricklewood Garage for the 16A's introduction in January 1976, being sent to Holloway in June 1978 following replacement by new B20s, and then to Thornton Heath two months later. It was exported to Hong Kong after withdrawal.

*Opposite above*: **Ten days** before it was withdrawn, never to run again, Holloway DMS24 passes Tufnell Park Station on the last leg of route 239's journey from Waterloo to Archway on 28 August 1982. When the route was withdrawn on 4 September, it was somewhat oddly being replaced between Archway and King's Cross by an extension of BL-operated route C11, originally a minibus service. The DMS had been another one that took part in their debut on route 220 from Shepherd's Bush Garage in January 1971, and another pilot overhaul, taking from December 1977 to June 1978 to complete.

*Opposite below*: **Despite being** almost six years newer than DMS24, West Ham DMS2193 was also withdrawn on 4 September 1982. In its final few days at London's service, on 28 August, it is at Stratford Broadway on circular route S1. It had entered service in December 1976 at Wood Green, moving to Seven Kings for RT replacement on route 148 in July 1977. It was displaced by Titans to West Ham in July 1980 and saw use with various operators after disposal by LT until 1994.

Dartmouth Park Hill
York Way Kings Cross
Euston Kingsway
239
ARCHWAY STATION
PLEASE PAY AS YOU ENTER
EGP 24J
TUFNELL
SCHOOL OF MOTORING
Embassy Number 1
West End
A400
Kentish Tow
Camden Tow
Kings Cros

STRATFORD
CIRCULAR
S1
UPTON PARK BOLEYN
PLEASE PAY AS YOU ENTER
OJD 193R
ALL ENQUIRIES

*Above*: **On 30** August 1982, just five days before its withdrawal, Putney DMS5 is at Roehampton War Memorial on route 85, on which DMSs had previously replaced the equally ill-fated SMSs. The blank advert spaces on its front are a sign of its impending demise. Route 85 would see operation by 'elderly' DMSs again briefly in the late 1980s, as part of the ill-fated Kingstonbus venture.

*Opposite above*: **On Bank** Holiday Monday 30 August 1982, following disturbances at the Notting Hill Carnival in previous years when conductors on routes serving the area were mugged and robbed of their fares income, doored buses were used as far as possible on them to offer a measure of protection to crews. Westbourne Park DM2571 is at Kensington Church turning into Kensington High Street on normally RM-operated route 52. It had been new to Brixton Garage in March 1978, moving to Westbourne Park (for route 18) upon replacement by RMs on routes 109 and 133 in August 1981. Sent south to Merton following replacement by new Metrobuses in October 1982, it lasted until May 1991, being scrapped thereafter.

*Opposite below*: **On the** same occasion, DM2550 likewise stands in for an RM on route 52A heading north along Kensington Church Street, bound for the heart of the 'danger area' where its garage is located. This route had been introduced just over a year previously, serving otherwise unserved roads between Ladbroke Grove and the new garage. Neither route 52 nor route 52A ever had scheduled DM/DMS allocations, both converting from RM to Metrobus OPO a few years later. This DM too, having entered service there in February 1978, was expelled from Brixton by RMs on routes 109 and 133, also moving to Westbourne Park for the 18 in August 1981. Following replacement by Metrobuses on that route, it was sent to Thornton Heath in April 1983, moving to Stockwell in July 1985 and lasting there until March 1991. It went for scrap shortly afterwards.

Neasden Willesden
Notting Hill Gate
Kensington Hyde Pk Cnr
52
VICTORIA
THX 571S

Best taste.
NESCAFÉ
Best buy!
52A
THX 550S
Distinctive Tri

*Above*: **As well** as earlier DMs and DMSs which had seen at best only six years or so in LT service, some much newer examples which had been in long-term store after mechanical or structural failures were permanently withdrawn from service as a result of the cuts. On 1 September 1982, three days before the cuts actually took place, B20 DM2596 and DM2630 are two of the most outrageous examples, having been cannibalised for spares and dumped with other withdrawn vehicles at the former A.E.C. Southall Works. Of these, the latter had entered service at Cricklewood in July 1978, transferring to Muswell Hill in August 1980 and expiring just four months later. DM2596's short service life was equally unimpressive, and both went for scrap early in 1983.

*Opposite above*: **On Friday** 3 September 1982, the 'eve of destruction' for so many of London's DMSs, Bexleyheath DMS1860 looks very smart when passing Sidcup Police Station on route 269. This route had been introduced in May 1977, replacing the inner section of route 229. This DMS had been new in June 1975 to Stamford Hill, already working at various other garages until overhauled in July 1981 to Bexleyheath. It was withdrawn in May 1983 upon replacement by new Titans, and never ran again.

*Opposite below*: **At almost** the same spot that day, Sidcup DMS2216 is working route 228, which had received them in place of RMs in January 1978, only eight months after conversion from RTs. This had been new to the garage in February 1977, and remained there until withdrawal in November 1982, also after replacement by Titans. It survived to see further use with various other operators until 2001, later being preserved.

CLIFF
NEWALBUM
269
BEXLEYHEATH GARAGE
CLIFF
NEWALBUM
726
GHM 860N
STATION ROAD

LIFE AS YOU LIKE IT...
228
CHISLEHURST
...AS A KELLY GIRL TEMP
Prudential FOR ALL YOUR INSURANCE
OJD 216R
Foots Cray A 211
BARCLAYS

*Above*: **Waiting to** turn right from Sidcup High Street into Station Road on route 21A on the same occasion, DMS2238 had been new to Seven Kings Garage replacing RTs on route 148 in July 1977, being displaced by new Titans to Sidcup three years later. It too was withdrawn upon replacement by them there in November 1982, and after a long period awaiting disposal saw further use as a non-PSV.

*Opposite above*: **On the** same day, Catford DMS1911 has been turned short on route 185 at Camberwell Green and sets off from Walworth Garage (originally Camberwell Tram Depot) for Blackwall Tunnel, Delta Metal Works in the evening rush hour. New to Potters Bar Garage in September 1975, it was transferred to Catford in November 1979, returning there after overhaul in August 1981. Displaced by Titans in September 1983, it was finally moved to New Cross, being withdrawn from there in January 1984.

*Opposite below*: **As dusk** falls that evening, Muswell Hill B20 DM2620 puts in a farewell performance on route 134 when passing Archway Station – replacing RMs have already begun to appear on the route as RM1805 on the left shows. This DM was new to Cricklewood in June 1978, displaced there by RMs on routes 16 and 16A in May 1980 and sent to Muswell Hill to replace earlier DMs. Following replacement by RMs on routes 43 and 134 the day after I took this picture and conversion for OPO, it was sent to Sutton Garage, surviving until November 1991. It was scrapped after that.

12
CAMBERWELL GREEN
London Transport
Vauxhall Camberwell
Dulwich Forest Hill
Catford Lewisham
185
BLACKWALL TUNNEL
PLEASE PAY AS YOU ENTER
KUC 911P
WLT 771

KING EDWARD
PANATELLAS
Friern Barnet
Muswell Hill Bdy
Camden Town
134
TOTTENHAM CT RD STN
KING EDWARD
PANATELLAS
134
EVITA
CHEAP DAY RETURN
805 DYE
THX620S

**Ample evidence** of the major changes that engulfed London's DMSs as a result of the Law Lords' service cuts on 4 September 1982 is this view of dozens of them in store at Ensign Bus's Purfleet yard twelve days later. LT did not have sufficient garage space to store so many dead vehicles. Of those nearest the camera, we have already encountered DMS392 (which survived to see a couple of years' post-LT use), but DMS207, which had entered service in December 1971 at Stamford Hill on the 67, and was overhauled in January 1979 to Putney Garage, ended up merely as a seat store for Midland Red East, who operated several of the type.

**Several dead** DMSs had already been stored at Ensign's for some time, as this forlorn group illustrates on the same occasion. DMS61, nearest the camera, had expired at Sidcup in February, having been overhauled there in September 1978. The two next to it have missing windscreens, though since the premises were patrolled by security guards with snapping Alsatian dogs, perhaps they are accident-damaged rather than vandalised. Such defunct vehicles were also a rich source of spare parts for those sold on for further use, though these, of course, went for scrap.